Grief, Grace,
and
Healing on the Drive

Also by the Same Author
In Between: At the Crossroads of Cultures (2021)

GRIEF, GRACE
&
Healing
on the Drive

Giddeon N. Angafor

SPEARS BOOKS

Denver, Colorado

Spears Books
An Imprint of Spears Media Press LLC
21699 E. Quincy Ave, Unit F #167
Aurora, CO 80015
United States of America

First Published in the United States of America in 2026 by Spears Books
www.spearsbooks.org
info@spearsmedia.com
Information on this title: https://spearsbooks.org/product/
grief-grace-and-healing-on-the-drive/

Publisher's Cataloging-in-Publication Data

Names: Angafor, Giddeon N., author.
Title: Grief, grace, and healing on the drive / Giddeon N. Angafor.
Description: Aurora, Colorado : Spears Books, 2026. | 130 pages ; 22 cm.
Identifiers: ISBN 9781957296838 (paperback) | ISBN 9781957296845 (ebook)
Subjects: LCSH: Angafor, Giddeon N. | Grief--Personal narratives. |
Bereavement--Personal narratives. | Loss (Psychology)--Personal narratives.
| Resilience (Personality trait) | Automobile driving--Psychological aspects. |
BISAC: BIOGRAPHY & AUTOBIOGRAPHY / Personal Memoirs. | FAMILY
& RELATIONSHIPS / Death, Grief, Bereavement. | PSYCHOLOGY / Grief &
Loss.
Classification: LCC BF575.G7 A54 2026 | DDC 155.9/37--dc23

Also available digitally on Kindle, Apple Books, and Google Books

Designed and typeset by Spears Media Press LLC
Cover design: D. Kambem

This book is dedicated to my son Davey-Jayce Angafor, my father and mother, Mr and Mrs Christopher, and Bertha Ndzamngang, my aunt, Mrs Bridget Mbuh Ngeh, uncle, Professor Amungwa Athanasius and my father-in-law, Bobe Michael Mbeng, all of blessed memory.

Contents

* * *

Foreword

When Giddeon first shared the idea for *Grief, Grace, and Healing on the Drive* with me, I realised it was more than just a book. It was a testimony, a lived journey, and a gift for anyone who has ever found themselves navigating the winding roads of loss. What struck me most was not simply the depth of grief he had endured, but the courage with which he chose to meet it with honesty, with faith, and with a willingness to keep driving forward even when the road seemed endless.

This work is not written from a distance. It is born from the passenger seat of real experience, from drives where silence spoke louder than words, and from moments when grace appeared unexpectedly, like sunlight breaking through the clouds. Giddeon does not pretend to have all the answers. Instead, he offers companionship, reflection, and the gentle reminder that healing is not about erasing pain but about learning to carry it differently.

What makes this book so powerful is its intimacy. It isn't a lecture or a manual; it's a conversation. As you read, you'll feel as if you're sitting beside a friend who understands, someone who has travelled the same path before you and is willing to share the lessons, struggles, and glimpses of hope seen along the way.

I believe *Grief, Grace and Healing on the Drive* will meet you wherever you are on your journey. It will not rush you, nor will it diminish the weight of your sorrow. Instead, it will remind you that grief is a reflection of love, that grace is always within reach, and that healing, though slow, can surprise us with its quiet strength.

It is my honour to present this book to you. May it act as a companion on your journey, and may you discover in its pages the courage to keep progressing, the grace to cherish each moment, and the healing that comes with time and faith.

Rev Fr Victor A Forgho

Preface

Every journey begins with a road. Some roads are smooth, lined with familiar landmarks and comforting scenery. Others are winding, unpredictable, and marked by loss, silence, and questions that seem to have no answers. *Grief, Grace, and Healing on the Drive* was born from such a road, a journey through the valleys of sorrow, the bends of resilience, and the long stretches where hope feels distant but never truly disappears.

I remember the first time I sat behind the wheel after loss had entered my life. The road stretched out before me, familiar yet strangely altered, as though grief had painted the landscape in muted colours. Every mile carried the weight of absence, and yet, it also bore the faint whisper of something else, grace, waiting quietly in the corners of my sorrow.

This book, *Grief, Grace, and Healing on the Drive*, is neither a manual nor a map with clear directions. It reflects the roads I have travelled, roads where silence pressed in, tears blurred the windscreen, and unexpected moments of peace reminded me that healing was possible. I write not as someone who has mastered grief, but as someone who has wrestled with it, sat with it, and learned to keep moving even when the journey felt unbearable. The purpose of this book is not to erase grief or rush healing. Instead, it is to offer companionship on the drive. Grief is not a detour; it is part of the map of our lives. Grace is the fuel that sustains us when the road feels endless. Healing is not a destination but a series of rest stops, moments when we gather strength, breathe deeply, and continue forward.

This book aims to remind readers that:

- Grief is universal: It affects every life, though each person's journey remains unique.
- Grace is transformative: it enables us to confront pain with compassion, both for ourselves and for others.
- Healing is possible: not through forgetting, but by learning to carry memory with gentleness instead of burden.

On the journey, there will be moments of reflection, stories that illuminate the human spirit, and practices that invite you to pause and find meaning even in the midst of loss. I hope that these pages serve as a guide, a companion, and a gentle reminder that you are not alone on the road. I wanted to share the road as I have seen it, so that you might feel less alone on yours. I cannot promise shortcuts or easy answers. What I can offer are stories, reflections, and gentle reminders that grief does not mean the end of the journey. Grace can meet us in the most unexpected places, and healing, though slow, can surprise us with its quiet arrival.

This book is for anyone navigating the landscape of grief, whether recent or long-standing, and seeking the grace that enables healing. It is a map based on lived experience, faith, and the quiet wisdom that arises when we venture to keep moving forward, even when the path feels uncertain.

I hope that as you read, you will find companionship in these words like a friend sitting in the passenger seat, not to take away the pain, but to remind you that you don't have to travel it alone.

Introduction

When the Road Became My Sanctuary

The road stretched before me like a lifeline. At first, it was only a means to escape the suffocating silence of rooms heavy with absence. But mile after mile, it became something else, a sanctuary, a moving temple where grief could breathe, sorrow could loosen its grip, and healing began to stir in the most unexpected ways.

Grief entered my life not just once but repeatedly, each time reshaping the contours of my existence. I held my young son in my arms as his breath faded, and in those two and a half hours after his death, the world collapsed into a silence too vast to comprehend. My father's passing came just as I was reaching the peak of my career and education, a moment when I longed to show him the fruits of my striving. Then came the loss of my job, at the very time my mother was unwell and needed me most. Redundancy became the backdrop to her eventual death, leaving me stripped of purpose and family all at once.

But the fractures did not end there. Long before these losses, I had already carried the ache of losing Mami Nta'ambang, my aunt and other mother, whose love had shaped my childhood and whose absence followed me across continents. As if that was not enough, nature had caused me to part ways with an in-law. Losing Bo Paul, my father-in-law, shook me in ways I never expected. His death didn't just leave a space at the table; it carved a hollow in my confidence, as though life had quietly removed another of the pillars I leaned on to measure the kind of father and man I hoped to be. It felt cruel, almost targeted, that someone who had become a compass for my own journey was suddenly gone. In the silence that followed, I found myself confronting not only grief but the unsettling question of how to keep moving when one of your guiding lights has been snatched away.

And just when I thought the road had taught me all it could about sorrow, the passing of my uncle, my mother's only surviving brother, a beacon of hope for our family and community, opened yet another wound. His death came at a time when reconciliation had finally blossomed between us, and we had begun to dream of a shared future, only for the road to bend sharply once more.

Each loss carved a new fault line, and together they created a landscape of brokenness. Home became a place where grief pressed against the walls and memories lingered like shadows. But the road was endless, unjudging, always moving, and offered something different.

I remember the feel of the steering wheel beneath my hands, its leather worn smooth by time, grounding me when everything else felt untethered. The engine's vibration beneath my seat was steady, a heartbeat reminding me I was still alive, still moving. The tyres hummed against the tarmac, a rhythm that echoed the pulse of my sorrow.

Landscapes shifted as I drove: fields unfurling in shades of green and gold, towns rising and fading in the rear-view mirror, forests standing as silent witnesses to my grief. Sometimes the road curved gently, as if cradling me in its arms; at other times it stretched straight and unending, daring me to keep going even when I longed to stop.

At night, the drives took on a different kind of holiness. The stars scattered across the sky like fragments of hope, distant yet luminous. The moon hung low, casting silver light on the road ahead, and I felt as though I were being guided by something greater than myself. Streetlights flickered past at intervals, marking time in a language only the road could speak. In those hours, when the world slept, I found a strange companionship in the vastness of the night.

There was a grace to these drives. The road did not demand that I be strong. It did not ask me to make sense of the chaos. It simply carried me forward, even when I had no destination in mind. In the solitude of long journeys, I began to notice small mercies: the way sunlight broke through clouds after rain, the way a familiar song on the radio echoed in my heart, the way distance offered a perspective I could not find in stillness. Healing did not arrive as a sudden revelation. It emerged slowly, like dawn breaking after a long night, in the quiet convergence of grief, uncertainty, and motion.

This book was born of those drives, of the countless hours when I wrestled with sorrow and discovered unexpected fragments of peace. From the sanctuary of the road, where grief and grace met, and healing began to whisper its presence.

And so, I ask the question that became the heartbeat of my journey: *Can healing happen in motion?*

CHAPTER 1

Two Hours, A Lifetime

When moments outweigh years, two hours become a lifetime.

When my son was placed in my arms, the world seemed to pause. The hospital room faded away, the voices became hushed, and all that remained was the delicate weight of him against my chest. We only had two hours, just two hours, to memorise the curve of his face, the softness of his skin, and the way his tiny fingers curled instinctively as if reaching for a life he would never hold. His mum was also fighting for her life, and the doctors were caring for her.

I recall leaning in close, whispering words that felt more like a prayer than speech.

I love you, DJ. I'm here. I wish I could give you the world, but I'll give you my heart instead.

His breath was faint, his presence fragile, but during those moments, I spoke to him as if he could hear every word. I told him about the dreams I had for him, the first steps, the first day at school, the laughter that would fill our home. I promised him that even if he could not stay, he would always belong.

The silence that followed his last breath was louder than any cry could have been. My arms, once full of promise, became empty vessels echoing the absence of what might have been. Grief struck me like a tidal wave, pulling me under. I had imagined a future full of scraped knees, bedtime stories, and teenage arguments. Instead, I was left with an empty car seat and a nursery that would never be used.

The drive home was a journey between two worlds. Outside the window, life continued as if nothing had changed. The sky was a gentle blue, streaked with clouds drifting lazily. Cars passed by, their drivers sipping coffee, listening to music, perhaps contemplating errands or meetings. The ordinary rhythm of the world felt cruel in its indifference. How could the sun still shine when mine had sunk?

Inside the car, my thoughts became a letter to DJ, our angel, just departed, with words spilling silently into the space between us:

"My boy, I wanted to bring you home with me. I wanted to carry you through the front door to show you the room we reserved just for you. Instead, I am carrying only your memory. The car seat is empty, but my heart is not. It is heavy with love, heavy with grief, heavy with the weight of what will never be.

I thought about the roads you might have travelled, the walk to school, the drive to college, the paths of a life never lived. I imagined the laughter that would have filled this car, the arguments over music, the quiet conversations on long drives. All of it vanished before it began, yet I feel it as if it were real.

DJ, I want you to know that you mattered. You mattered in those two hours, and you still do. You will always matter. Your life was brief, but it was never small. You taught me that love can be infinite even when time is not. You taught me that peace is not found in forgetting, but in remembering with grace."

The world outside was lively, bustling with activity and colour. Children walked hand in hand with their parents, shopkeepers opened their doors, and buses roared past. Yet inside me, everything was subdued, drained of colour. It was as if I were passing through a painting I could no longer touch, separated by a glass pane between the living and the mourning.

And yet, even in that unbearable contrast, there was grace. Grace in the way the road stretched ahead, reminding me that movement was still possible even when my heart felt stuck. Grace in the rhythm of the tyres, a quiet lullaby that carried me through the storm. Grace in the thought that my son's brief life had left me with a love so profound it could not be undone, even by death.

As I reflect on his passing, I realise that finding peace has not been about forgetting. It has been about learning to carry him with me in a different way. His absence is a shadow, but his memory is a light. I hold onto the truth that his life, though brief, was not meaningless. He mattered. He mattered to me, to us, to the world that will never know him but will always feel the ripple of his existence through the love he left behind.

The journey goes on. Some days, the road feels unbearably long; other days, it feels like a quiet companion. Grief accompanies me, but so does grace. And somewhere between these two, I catch fleeting glimpses of peace, moments when I can breathe, moments when I smile at the memory of holding him, moments when I realise that even two hours can contain a lifetime of love.

CHAPTER 2

The Silence After Goodbye

People talk about closure, but they don't mention that it is a myth. There is only the ache and the slow realisation that life will never be the same.

The phone rang, and with it came the second fracture. My brother's voice carried the weight of news that would shatter my world. His words were simple, yet they struck like stones: Dad is gone.

For a moment, there was a stiff silence, as if the air itself refused to move. Then came the scream, raw and guttural, a sound I did not realise I was capable of making. Nooooo! It tore through the room, yet even that cry could not undo what had already happened. What followed was quieter, more devastating: silent sobs, tears falling without sound, the kind that hollows you out from within.

My wife held me as I wept, her tears mingling with mine. Her arms were a fragile refuge from an endless storm. I remember the scent of her favourite perfume on her pyjamas, the feel of the fabric against my cheek, and the warmth of her body pressed close to mine. These small details became anchors in a moment when everything else was falling apart.

In my mind, I visualised the sterile hospital corridors where my dad took his last breath. I imagined the rhythmic beeping of machines, each pulse taunting my hope, until the sound finally gave way to silence. That silence was not peaceful; it was final. It is the kind of silence that fills every corner, leaving no room for denial.

Later, I stood by the window, looking out at a world that carried on as if nothing had happened. Cars drove down the street, neighbours took their dogs for walks, and the sun followed its usual course across the sky. Outside, life seemed normal. Inside, everything had fallen apart. My father's absence left a gap that swallowed the familiar, leaving me confused in a world that no longer felt like mine.

Grief introduced me to strange rituals. In my mind, I found myself staring at his empty chair, imagining him seated there, his posture relaxed, his eyes fixed on me with that quiet attentiveness he always carried. I traced the dent his body had left in the cushion, longing for one more conversation, one more laugh, one more piece of advice. The chair became both a shrine and a wound, a reminder of presence and absence, intertwined.

People speak of closure as if it were a destination, a neat ending to the story of loss. But closure is a myth. Grief lingers like an echo that never fades. It reverberates through ordinary moments, in smells that remind me of him, the sound of his favourite song, the texture of his old jacket hanging in the wardrobe, and the sound of his laughter or voice calling out to his grandchildren. Each sensory detail pulls me back, reminding me that love does not vanish with death.

My father imparted lessons that still influence me: the value of hard work, the importance of kindness, and the strength that comes from humility. Yet his death left questions unanswered, things I never asked, stories I never heard, and wisdom I never received. Those questions linger like unfinished sentences, reminders of conversations we will never have.

This was the second fracture, and in that moment, I realised that grief is not just about losing someone; it's about losing the version of yourself that existed when they were alive. My identity shifted in the silence after goodbye. I was no longer simply a son; I was a son without a father. It even felt a bit frightening to realise that my generation was gradually stepping up to the fathers, the traditional elders of the new generation. Grief reshaped me, carving new contours into my life and forcing me to carry both the ache of absence and the grace of memory.

And so, I live with the echo. It does not fade but teaches me. It reminds me that love is stronger than silence, that memory can be both a burden and a gift, and that the ache itself proves how deeply he mattered.

The days after my father's death blurred together, each heavy with the weight of absence. Time lost its rhythm. Morning and night felt indistinguishable, as if grief had swallowed the clock. I moved through those hours in a daze, performing tasks that felt both necessary and impossible, calling relatives, replying to condolences, and making arrangements. Each word spoken was a reminder that he was gone, and each repetition of the news reopened the wound.

The house became a strange museum of memories. His shoes by the door, his coat draped over the chair, the faint scent of his aftershave lingering in the hallway. These ordinary objects became sacred relics, each bearing the texture of his presence. I would pause at his chair, gazing at the dent his body had left, imagining him sitting there, ready to share one of his quiet observations or a story from his youth. The longing for one more conversation was unbearable.

The funeral was both a ritual of comfort and of cruelty. Comfort came from bringing together those who loved him, who spoke his name with reverence, and who shared stories that reflected the breadth of his life. Cruelty lay in making his absence undeniable. Even more distressing was that it occurred during the COVID-19 pandemic, amid the crisis in the Northwest and Southwest regions of Cameroon, where safety could not be guaranteed. It meant things had to be hurried so we could escape danger sooner. Despite this, I remember the scent of lilies, heavy and sweet, filling the church altar where the funeral took place. I recall the sound of hymns rising, voices trembling with emotion. I feel the polished wood beneath my hand as I touch the coffin, knowing it was the last time I would be close to him in this world.

There was a moment during the service when silence fell, and I felt it again, the silence that had followed his last breath. It was a silence that carried both finality and reverence, as if to say: This is the end of his story here, but not the end of his presence in you.

After the funeral, people spoke of closure, as if the ritual had smoothed the edges of grief. But closure is a myth. The ache lingered, echoing like a sound that refused to fade. Grief did not end with the burial; it began again. It followed me home, into the quiet of my room, into the spaces where his voice used to be.

During that period, I came to understand grief as something far more complex than sorrow. It wasn't just an emotion I carried; it was a force that reshaped the contours of my identity. Losing my father didn't simply make me a son in mourning; it made me a son without a father, and that distinction altered the way I moved through the world. The shift was subtle at first, but profound, as if a quiet line had been drawn between who I had been and who I was becoming.

Grief redrafted the map of my life. It introduced new boundaries, new silences, new depths I hadn't known existed. It demanded that I learn to hold two truths at once: the persistent ache of absence and the unexpected grace of memory. In that tension, I discovered that grief isn't only about what is lost; it's also about what remains, how love continues to echo, how identity continues to evolve, and how we learn to inhabit a world that has been permanently changed.

I reflected on the lessons my father had taught me: the dignity of hard work, the importance of listening more than speaking, and the quiet strength of humility. These lessons became lifelines, threads of him woven into me. Yet alongside them were questions left unanswered, things I never asked, stories I never heard, and wisdom I never received. Those questions hovered like unfinished sentences, reminders of the conversations we will never have.

The rituals of grief, the funeral, the condolences, and the quiet moments alone did not bring closure. Instead, they brought recognition. Recognition that grief is not something to be solved but something to live with. Recognition that love does not vanish with death but transforms into memory, into longing, and into the ache that shapes who we become.

And so, I carry him with me. In the silence after goodbye, in the echo that lingers, and in the lessons that remain. Grief is not a door that closes; it is a shadow that walks beside me, a reminder that love, once given, never truly leaves.

CHAPTER 3

The Bend in the Road I Never Saw Coming

Here, I return to the father-uncle whose light guided me, and whose loss reshaped my drive toward healing.

The drive through grief is never a straight path. It twists without warning, dips into valleys we thought we had already crossed, and rises into hills that test the strength of our breath. Some turns reveal unexpected beauty; others confront us with losses we were never prepared to face. And then there are the bends that take someone from us just when we had begun to find our way back to them.

Losing my uncle, Professor Amungwa, my mother's only surviving brother, her last sibling from the same womb, was one such bend. It was sharp, sudden, and devastating. Even now, as I look back on that stretch of the journey, I feel the jolt of it in my chest. To me, he was more than an uncle. He was a beacon, steady, brilliant, and far-reaching. Prof was equally a devoted father to his children, a steadfast pillar of faith and discipline, yet always a gentle and loving provider for his wife and children. His presence shaped their lives with wisdom, strength, and a quiet tenderness remembered with deep gratitude. To the community, he was a pillar. To the country, he was a mind of rare distinction, a scholar whose work shaped conversations and opened doors for many. But to my mother, he was something even deeper: her other son, her brother, her father, and her companion in survival.

They had lost their parents young. They had buried elder siblings before they were old enough to understand the cruelty of fate. And through it all, she had stood by him, supporting him, encouraging him, watching him toil through hardship to become the man the world would later celebrate. Their bond was forged in shared loss and strengthened by shared resilience.

Throughout his life, my uncle leaned on my mother with a trust that ran deeper than ordinary siblinghood. She had become, in many ways, the mother he never truly had the chance to know or bond with, a steady source of guidance, protection, and unconditional loyalty. In moments of uncertainty, he turned to her; in seasons of triumph, he shared his joy with her first. Their bond was shaped by loss but strengthened by devotion, and she carried him through life with the quiet, unwavering love of a mother who had chosen her child twice, once by birth, and again by sacrifice. After my father passed, that bond deepened even further. My mother leaned on him as one leans on a trusted pillar, her brother, her son, her husband in spirit, her last link to the family she once knew.

Yet life, in its complexity, does not always follow the script of affection. When I travelled to Europe, a rift widened between my uncle and me. Assumptions were made about me, and important decisions I had made about my life and the direction of travel led to an exchange of words. Misunderstandings hardened, and for a time, I did not speak to the man who had been a father figure to me in my childhood. I literally grew up with the man around my family compound. During his holidays, whether returning from the Agric School in Bambui, the University of Yaoundé or later from his studies in the UK, he lived with us in the family compound. He became a steady presence, one who shaped the daily lives of both my elder brother and I. He guided and directed us with patience and purpose, always urging us to study hard, aim high, and become something meaningful in life. His influence reached far beyond ordinary uncle duties, leaving a legacy of discipline, encouragement, and deep care.

But even in that silence created by the misunderstanding and subsequent rift, I admired him. Quietly and secretly, I lived by the very principles he embodied: hard work, truth, discipline, and the relentless pursuit of academic excellence. His life was a testament to what determination could build, and though I never proudly shouted that out loud, I carried his lessons with me across continents.

Families fall out. Hearts bruise. But love, when it is real, finds its way back as it did with my uncle and me. At my father's funeral, which is where I last met my uncle after a while, something shifted. Grief has a way of stripping us down to our truest selves. In that rawness, we found each other again. We grieved together, talked intimately, embraced each other, and allowed the years of distance to dissolve into moments of intimacy shared between a son and his father-uncle. It felt like reclaiming a father I had lost twice, once through conflict, and once through silence.

We spoke of the future with excitement. We dreamed aloud about collaborating on a book project, his wisdom, my pen, our shared heritage woven into something lasting. For the first time in a long time, I felt the fullness of the African spirit of kinship: an uncle who was also a father, a mentor, a guide I could finally turn to.

The road ahead looked promising. But life, unpredictable as ever, had other plans. Not long after my father's burial, my uncle took ill. The treatments were gruelling, expensive, and often included painful blood transfusions in a hospital miles away from his hometown. Still, we held onto hope. The doctors were optimistic. He was responding well. We began making plans again. He was due to travel to the UK for his son's deaconate and priestly ordinations. We were excited to welcome him to the UK to celebrate together. I was personally looking forward to continuing the healing and cementing the reconciliation that had begun between us at my dad's funeral.

But his visa arrived late. Too late. He could not travel for the deaconate. Instead, he called me and asked me to stand in for him, to play father to my cousin on that sacred day. I accepted with pride, honoured to carry his mantle, unaware that this would be the last responsibility he would ever entrust to me.

We told ourselves we would make up for it during the priestly ordination. We imagined a bigger gathering, a joyful reunion, a celebration of faith and family. But the road bent again. His health deteriorated. The treatments that once seemed promising could no longer hold back the tide. And before we could gather again, before he could see the ordination, before we could start work on the project to write that book, he was gone.

His passing in 2023 shattered me. I grieved not only for the man he was, but also for the time we lost during our falling-out. I mourned the conversations we never had, the wisdom I never received, the collaboration on a book that would never be written. I mourned the father I had regained only to lose again.

He had achieved so much, academically, socially, and personally. A celebrated professor. A community leader and noble of the Bambui Fondom. A humane soul whose brilliance never overshadowed his kindness. To lose such a man felt like losing a library, a lighthouse, a legacy.

Looking back now, I believe that letting go of grudges is one of the quietest but most powerful acts of self-preservation. Resentment, I realised, weighs heavily, often burdening the one who carries it far more than the one who caused the hurt. Life is simply too short to keep replaying old wounds or allowing past moments to shape the present. Releasing a grudge isn't about excusing what happened; it's about choosing peace over bitterness and freeing oneself to move forward with a lighter heart.

And when reconciliation is possible, it brings a kind of grace that can't be forced or faked. Meeting someone again with openness rather than armour creates space for healing, sometimes for both sides. When this happens, it reminds us that people can grow, that relationships can be mended, and that forgiveness can restore what anger erodes. Even small steps toward understanding can soften the sharp edges of the past. In the end, letting go and, where possible, reconciling isn't just an act of kindness toward others; it's a profound gift of freedom and renewal to oneself.

This explains why even in the ache, grace found me. It came to mind in the memory of the reconciliatory embrace with my uncle at my father's funeral. It came in the knowledge that we made peace, that we looked to the future with hope, that we ended our story not in bitterness but in reconciliation.

Healing, I have learned, is not the absence of pain. It is the ability to look back on the journey and see not only the losses, but also the moments of grace that softened them.

My uncle's life was one such grace.

Our reconciliation was another.

And the drive continues, with him now a quiet compass in my heart, guiding me through each bend I never saw coming.

CHAPTER 4

The Steady Hand On the Wheel

*The family was a vehicle with many seats, and he made sure
every one of them was filled with love.*

Some people join the journey not at the starting line, but somewhere along the highway, yet somehow it feels like they've been in the car with you from the very beginning. My father-in-law, Bo Paul, was one of those rare souls. He didn't just welcome me into his family; he opened the door wide, shifted over, and made space for me with a warmth that needed no explanation.

Bo Paul had that same quiet strength I admired in my own father, the kind of presence that steadies a vehicle even when the road beneath it is cracked and unpredictable. A calmness that didn't need to be announced. An integrity that didn't need to be proven. He simply was. One thing I continue to cherish about my father-in-law is that he shaped me in ways I never expected. He accepted me as I was, but he also quietly modelled the kind of steadiness and strength that helped me grow into a calmer, more grounded, more confident version of myself. He never pushed, never preached; he is the kind of model that simply lived with a gentleness and assurance that made you want to rise to meet it.

Through his example, I learned that real confidence doesn't shout, it settles. That calm isn't weakness, it's wisdom. And that being part of a family isn't just about being included, but being encouraged to become better. To say he accepted me is true, but it doesn't go far enough. He helped mould me, patiently, subtly, and with a kindness that leaves a lasting mark. And for that, I'll always be grateful.

He had his special seat outside the house. Whenever I visited him, I always knew where I would find him. Before I even stepped out of the car, before the dust settled behind me, I could already picture him: sitting in his favourite chair outside the main building. That chair wasn't just furniture; it was a throne of sorts, a lookout point, a command centre. From there, he watched the world with the quiet authority of a man who had lived enough life to understand what mattered and what didn't.

He sat with a posture that was both relaxed and imposing, as though he carried the weight of his years with dignity rather than burden. His hands, strong, weathered, steady, rested on the armrests like they were holding the edges of a steering wheel only he could see. And when he saw me approaching, his face would soften into that familiar half-smile, the one that said, 'You're home. Come sit.'

I would walk up to him, and he would tilt his head slightly, studying me the way a seasoned driver studies the horizon, patiently, knowingly, scanning for subtle signs, reading the weather of my mood, sensing the twists and turns of the journey I had taken to get there. In that brief pause, before a word was spoken, he seemed to understand more about me than I had managed to put into sentences. It was as if he could read the road behind my eyes, noticing the things I tried to hide and the things I didn't yet know how to say.

"Ah, Bo Les," he would say, his voice low and warm. "You are welcome." And in that moment, I always felt like I had arrived somewhere safe. Even when I travelled back to Europe, the distance never dimmed his presence. I would call him sometimes late in the evening, when the house was quiet, and the children were asleep, or in those rare pockets of calm when they had gone to school or out to play. The line would ring, and then his familiar voice would come through, steady, unhurried, like a man who had all the time in the world.

He never rushed a conversation. He listened the way some people watch a sunset: patiently, with full attention, as though nothing else mattered until the colours had settled. Sometimes he would laugh softly before he spoke, as if amused that I had bothered to call at all. Other times, he would slip into a story, one of those gentle, winding tales that didn't need a point because the pleasure was in the telling. And even across continents, I could feel the same ease I felt standing beside him in person, the sense that, for those few minutes, I was exactly where I was meant to be.

"Bo Paul," I would greet him. "Ah, my son," he would reply, the words carrying that same acceptance he had shown me from the first day. "How is life on that side of the world?" "It's good," I would say. "Cold sometimes. Busy. But good." He would chuckle softly. "Cold is good. It keeps you sharp. And the children? My grandchildren, how are they?" "They're growing fast," I'd tell him. "You wouldn't believe how tall they're getting." "I believe it," he'd say. "Children grow like the road stretches, quietly, steadily, before you realise how far you've come."

Sometimes he would ask about their school, their friends, their little habits, including whether they knew about their cultural roots. Other times, he would simply listen, humming in acknowledgement, letting me speak freely, as though my words were stones I could set down one by one. He never rushed the conversation. He never made me feel like I was calling out of obligation or ticking off a duty. Instead, he treated every call like a visit, like I had just walked up to his chair again, dust on my shoes and a story to tell.

There was always that same gentle pause before he answered, the same warmth in his voice that made even the most ordinary updates feel worth sharing. He had a way of making distance feel irrelevant, as if the miles between us folded neatly away the moment he picked up. And in those small, unhurried exchanges, he reminded me, without ever saying it, that family isn't measured in proximity, but in presence. And when the call ended, he always said the same thing: "Stay well, my son, and take care of yourself, my children and their mother. Take care of the road beneath you each time you are out in the car."

He came from humble beginnings, the kind of starting point where the road is more potholes than pavement. But he refused to let that be the story's end. He worked, he sacrificed, he pushed forward with a determination that wasn't loud or boastful. It was quiet, persistent, like a car that keeps moving even when the fuel gauge is low. He wanted better for his children. Not just his blood children, but the ones who married into the family. The ones who arrived later. The ones like me. He never drew lines. Never separated. Never said "these are mine" and "these are others." To him, family was a vehicle with many seats, and he made sure every one of them was filled with love, guidance, and opportunity.

As life would have it, illness came to Bo Paul like the final bend in the road. When illness came, it didn't take away his dignity. If anything, it revealed it more clearly. He carried his pain the way he carried everything else, with grace, with patience, with that same steady hand on the wheel. He didn't complain. He didn't dramatise. He simply adjusted his speed, shifted gears, and kept going. But eventually, the road took a turn we couldn't follow. The day he left us, it felt like the engine of the whole family had gone quiet. The chair outside the main building sat empty, and the silence around it was louder than any words.

The day we received the news felt like the car of our lives skidded violently off the road. My wife's scream cut through the house with a force I had never heard from her before, a raw, breaking sound that came from somewhere deep in her soul. She doubled over, clutching her stomach as though the grief itself had reached inside and twisted something vital. I rushed to her, holding her as tightly as I could, feeling her body shake against mine. And in that moment, it wasn't just her father we were mourning. His passing came barely a year after my own father's, and the grief hit us like a collision we never saw coming. We cried together, loud, helpless, aching tears, lamenting that we had both lost the men who had shaped us, guided us and welcomed us. Two fathers gone. Two fathers-in-law gone. It felt as though the pillars on both sides of our family had fallen at once, leaving us exposed on an open road with no guardrails. The sorrow was doubled, layered, intertwined, and all we could do was hold each other and let the storm pass through us.

Grief made me pull over, and it caused me to sit in the stillness. The same grief made me look at the empty seat beside me and feel its ache. But healing, slow, gentle, persistent, reminded me that my father-in-law hadn't left the car entirely. His lessons were still in the glove compartment. His voice still echoed in the rear-view mirror. His fingerprints were still on the steering wheel.

I found healing in carrying him forward. Every time I choose kindness over judgment, I hear him. Every time I steady myself in a storm, I feel him. Every time I make room for someone else in my life's vehicle, I honour him. He may no longer be sitting in that chair outside the main building, but he is still with me, guiding, steadying, reminding me to drive well.

And so, I continue the journey, carrying him not as a shadow but as a co-driver whose wisdom will always shape the road ahead.

CHAPTER 5

Redundancy, the Invisible Loss

When I lost my job, it felt like losing the last part of myself.
Who was I without the title, the payslip, the routine?

Grief does not always wear black. Sometimes it arrives in an email titled: "Meeting Request." That was how my third loss came, not with tears and funerals, but through a sterile HR conversation lasting less than sixty minutes. It was the silence of an HR office, the kind that hums with awkwardness, where words are chosen carefully and delivered with rehearsed sympathy.

I sat across the table, listening to phrases like "restructuring," "the business is struggling," "we are merging departments and some posts are no longer required," and "we appreciate your contribution." Each phrase was a polite dagger, slicing through the identity I had built over the years. As they spoke, my mind drifted in and out of the room. Part of me was still trying to decode their carefully chosen words, while another part was already racing ahead, wondering what I would tell my family, what this might mean for the rent or mortgage, whether my colleagues already knew, and whether I should have seen this coming. A strange mix of embarrassment and disbelief settled in my chest, as if I had somehow failed a test I didn't know I was taking.

I entered that room as an employee, a contributor, a man with a title. I had walked in with a sense of place, of purpose, of being needed. But with each sentence, that sense loosened, thread by thread. By the time they slid the envelope across the table, I felt hollowed out, as someone had quietly removed the scaffolding that held me upright. I left stripped of it all, carrying only my coat, a folder of "next steps," and the unsettling feeling that the ground beneath me had shifted while I wasn't looking.

The meeting ended quickly, as these things often do. There was no ceremony, no farewell worthy of the hours, effort, and sacrifices, just a quiet nod, a stack of papers, and the odd walk back to my desk. Packing up felt like a betrayal of everything I had invested in that place. The hum of computers, the shuffle of colleagues avoiding eye contact, the sterile smell of office carpet, all of it mocked the reality that I was no longer part of this world.

Walking out of the building was stranger still. The door clicked shut behind me with the same indifferent sound it made every other day, but this time it felt final, almost cruel. The air outside seemed too normal for what had just happened. Cars passed, people hurried by, life continued with no awareness that mine had just been knocked off its axis. I stood there for a moment, holding a box that suddenly felt heavier than it should, wondering where exactly I was supposed to go next.

My mind swung between numbness and panic. One moment, I was telling myself it was just a job, that people go through this all the time. Next, I was replaying every decision I'd made in the last year, searching for the misstep that might have saved me. I thought about my family, how I would explain it, how I would reassure them when I wasn't sure how to reassure myself. There was a quiet shame too, the kind that creeps in even when you know you've done nothing wrong. A sense of being exposed, as though everyone could see the gap where your confidence used to be.

As I walked to the car, each step felt like it belonged to someone else. I kept expecting the shock to break, for anger or clarity or something solid to take its place. But all I felt was the hollow echo of a chapter closing without warning. Processing it wasn't a single moment; it was a slow, uneven acceptance that the ground had shifted, and I would need time to find my footing again. And in that in-between space, between what was and what would come next, I realised that losing a job isn't just about employment. It's about identity, belonging, and the quiet work of rebuilding yourself when no one is watching.

The word 'redundancy' is cruel. It doesn't just mean your job is gone; it implies that you are unnecessary, surplus, and easily replaced. I remember sitting in my car afterwards, staring at the dashboard, feeling the weight of that word pressing on my chest. Losing my son, then my father, had shattered my heart, but losing my job had fractured my sense of identity. Who was I without the routine, the purpose, and when the future becomes uncertain? The days that followed dissolved into a fog of uncertainty. I quietly packed away my desk; each item was a reminder of years spent building something that no longer mattered. The framed photo of my team, our team-building exercises, and the notebooks filled with ideas I had planned to implement all suddenly seemed pointless. I carried the box to my car, feeling as if I was moving the remnants of a life that had vanished overnight.

The timing made the loss feel even heavier. My mother was critically ill, constantly in and out of the hospital. Each conversation with her carried its own grief and fear of losing her. Now, on top of that, there was the shame of unemployment. I felt I was failing on every front, unable to provide, protect, or hold my life together. I harboured several fears, including the unknown, not being good enough, and never finding my way back. These fears led me to hide the redundancy from my mum, for fear it might worry her and hasten her decline.

It felt surreal to shift between these worlds: the office where my identity was dismantled and the hospital where my mother's body was failing. In one space, I was stripped of my role, my salary, my routine; in the other, I was robbed of certainty, watching the woman who had given me life fight to hold onto hers. The clash of grief and career loss was unyielding.

I wrestled with fear, including fear of bills mounting, fear of interviews that never materialised, and fear of being stuck in a cycle of loss. But beneath the fear was something deeper: shame, a quiet companion in redundancy. It seeped into conversations, causing me to avoid certain questions and almost hesitate when someone asked, "So, what do you do for work?" I felt it when I spoke to the nurses and answered questions from relatives about work and life. It made me question my worth, feeling that I was not strong enough, smart enough, or valuable enough to keep my place. It took months to realise that redundancy was not a verdict on my worth; it was a detour, a painful, unexpected detour that would lead me down a road I never imagined travelling.

Redundancy is an invisible grief. People don't send flowers or write sympathy cards. They say things like, "You'll bounce back," or "It's just a job." But it's never just a job. It's the rhythm of your days, the structure of your weeks, the sense of belonging that anchors you. When that disappears, the silence is deafening.

Looking back now, I see that this loss, like the others, brought a strange gift. It forced me to confront the question I had been avoiding: What really matters? Not titles, not salaries, not the illusion of security, but peace, purpose, and grace. I did not know it then, but the road ahead, the literal road, would become the classroom where I learned those lessons.

Redundancy, especially the death of my mother while I was unemployed, forced me to redefine success. It was no longer about promotions or performance reviews. Success, it became clear, was about endurance, about showing up for my mother in her hospital room, even if it meant emptying the little savings I had set aside for rainy days. It was about facing the mirror without turning away; it meant finding meaning in the small acts of living when the big structures had collapsed.

Preparing for her funeral was something I did reluctantly, almost mechanically. Discussing what clothes to dress mum in for her final journey, choosing flowers, arranging hymns, speaking with the priest, all of it felt surreal, as though I was watching someone else's life unfold. Yet in those rituals, I began to see threads of resilience. Each decision, each step forward, was proof that even in the deepest grief, we find ways to keep moving.

I remember standing at her graveside, the cold air biting my skin, the smell of smoke and spices from the cooking for her funeral heavy in the air. My heart was shattered, but in that moment, I realised that grief and resilience are not opposites; they are companions. Grief reminds us of what we have lost; resilience reminds us of what we still carry.

The intersection of grief and career loss was a double blow, yet it revealed something profound: grief extends beyond death. It can manifest in the loss of identity, the collapse of stability, and the quiet dismantling of the life you believed you had built. Nevertheless, within that dismantling lies the possibility of rebuilding not the same life but a new one, shaped by resilience, carved by survival, and defined by a deeper understanding of what truly matters.

The lessons of redundancy and my mother's passing during a period of unemployment began to intertwine. Losing my job prompted me to question my identity beyond titles. Losing my mother while out of work forced me to contemplate my sense of self beyond family roles. Together, these losses transformed me, fostering a new understanding of purpose.

I began to see that success was not about climbing ladders or clinging to routines. Success was about endurance, love, and showing up even when everything inside me wanted to collapse. It was about honouring my mother's lessons, her quiet strength, her unwavering care, and carrying them forward into the way I lived.

Grief became the soil in which resilience grew. Redundancy taught me that identity can be rebuilt. My mother's passing taught me that love endures beyond death. Together, they prepared me for the next chapter of my life, a chapter where grief, resilience, and purpose are not separate threads, but a single woven fabric.

I was no longer the person I had been before these losses. I was someone remade by them, someone who understood that life is fragile, identity is fluid, and purpose is found not in job titles or routines, but in the way we carry love forward.

And so, I stepped into the next chapter not without scars, not without ache, but with a new identity shaped by survival, softened by grief, and strengthened by resilience.

CHAPTER 6

When My World Stopped Again

Grief does not come in waves; it comes in storms. And when the third storm hit, I was not sure I would survive.

The first time death and ultimately grief came, it rocked me; the second time, it shattered me. But the third time, it hollowed me out completely. Losing my son was the first storm that had already left me battered, leaving a scar that was nearing the end of the healing process. Losing my father felt like the ground had been pulled from beneath me, and I had only just begun to learn how to walk again on unsteady legs. His passing left a wound that was still raw, still bleeding. Then came the loss of my job during my mother's illness, carrying a double burden: not only the practical blow of redundancy but also the emotional weight of being unable to support her as I wished.

That kind of loss leaves one feeling powerless, suspended between grief and responsibility, with the road ahead clouded by uncertainty. But before I could find balance, before I could breathe without the ache of my dad's absence, and the loss of my job, the third blow, or rather, a major punch, came: my mother's passing.

My mum's passing was not just another loss. It was the collapse of the last pillar holding up the fragile structure of my world. Suddenly, I was not only grieving a parent, but mourning the end of a family, the silence of a home that once held laughter, arguments, and the comforting rhythm of everyday life. She had been our rallying presence, the steady heartbeat of the family. Always urging us to stay united, to look out for one another, to show care and concern even when we disagreed. She believed fiercely in togetherness. To her, siblings were not optional relationships; they were life-long responsibilities.

She had this way of balancing tenderness with firmness. She would wrap you in warmth when you needed comfort, but she would also call you out without hesitation when you stepped out of line. She didn't believe in letting things fester. If someone behaved badly, she addressed it. If someone was hurting, she noticed. If someone drifted away, she reached for them. She guarded the extended family like a mother hen, always counting her chicks, making sure each one was accounted for, physically, emotionally, and spiritually. No one slipped through the cracks on her watch.

Her presence was a kind of quiet authority, the sort that didn't need to be announced. You just felt it. She held the family together not through grand gestures, but through the small, consistent acts of love that stitched us into something whole. And when she left, it wasn't just a gap; it was a crater. The kind of absence that echoes.

Her departure was a devastating blow, not only to us but to the entire community. People who had leaned on her, confided in her, sought her wisdom, suddenly found themselves without the person who had always made time, always listened, always cared. But for us, her children and our extended family, the loss cut even deeper. It felt as though the compass that had guided us all our lives had suddenly vanished, leaving us to navigate grief, responsibility, and adulthood without the one person who had always known how to steady the ship.

Losing her meant losing the person who believed in us most, who held us to account, who reminded us of who we were and who we were meant to be. And in the quiet that followed her passing, we realised just how much of our strength had come from her, how much of our unity had been shaped by her hands, her voice, her unwavering love.

I remember receiving the news around 12:10 am USA time via a text message from my older brother. I believe he avoided calling because of the time difference, knowing I was in the USA visiting our younger brother with my family. I stared at the phone for about a minute, my hands greasy from chicken fat, as I was marinating for my brother's graduation party the next day. I also recall going quiet for a while, almost dazed, as I gazed at the white wall in front of me, and I could hear the words echoing in my ears like a cruel joke.

Then I turned to my younger brother, whom I knew would be devastated by the news, and revealed the shocking message to him. It was meant to be his big day, but he had to be told that our last remaining giant was no more. At that moment, still weeping and trying to comfort my brother, who, like me, had sunk to the floor with our wives scrambling over us, I asked myself: How could life be so relentless? How could the world take away both anchors that held me steady?

The days that followed blurred into a whirlwind of paperwork, condolences, and silence. Silence, the kind that presses against your chest until breathing becomes labour. My siblings and I arranged the funeral, following her final instructions exactly as she would have wished. My sisters and brothers at home moved through Mum's bedroom like ghosts, touching the things she touched, inhaling the lingering scent of her perfume on a scarf.

Every object held a memory, and every memory felt like a knife. Sorting through her belongings was both a ritual and a torment. Each suitcase contained fragments of her life: scarves folded neatly, uniforms from her various church and community groups packed tidily, letters tucked away, photographs faded and greyed by time. When I reached her room, I lingered over her clothes, pressing them to my face and inhaling the faint scent still clinging to the fabric. It was the closest I could get to holding her again. Her clothes were folded slowly, as if folding time itself, as if we could tuck away the ache with each crease.

The house, once alive with her presence, became painfully silent. The silence was not calming; it was stifling. Every creak of the floor or opening of cupboards reminded us of her absence. I would find myself listening for her footsteps, her voice calling my name, only to be met with emptiness.

Grief changes shape when it returns. The first time, it was sharp and raw, slicing through each moment with unbearable clarity. The second time, it was heavier and more complex, like carrying a stone that grows larger with each step. It was not just sadness; it was exhaustion. Mourning again felt like reopening a wound that had barely begun to scar. It made me remember what my wife often says from her academic knowledge and personal experience of grief: that it is not linear. It does not come in neat stages as the books suggest. It arrives in storms, violent, unpredictable, and merciless. One moment you're numb; the next, you're drowning in tears you did not realise you still had. I found myself crying in the kitchen, in the car, in the middle of a supermarket aisle because a song, an object, or a thought reminded me of mum. The world felt hostile, filled with reminders of what I had lost.

All these episodes made me realise that grief is not static. It evolves, mutates, and becomes harder to articulate. With my mother's passing, it was no longer a flood of tears. Instead, it settled into a dull ache, a numbness that spread through my days. Tears stopped flowing, not because the pain had lessened, but because it had become too heavy to lift into words or sobs.

I found myself grieving not only for my mother but also for the family I no longer had. It frightened me that I was slowly becoming one of the last anchors, the final witness to memories that now existed only within me. That realisation was lonelier than death itself. Moreover, it occurred to me that there would be no mother to ask for advice, no one to share the small victories or the crushing defeats. Loneliness became a constant companion, whispering in the quiet hours of the night. I tried to pray, but even my prayers felt heavy, like stones sinking in deep water. Being the last family anchor meant Mum carried memories that only she and her siblings could boast of. Holidays became hollow, traditions faded, and the stories that once united us now only echoed in my mind. Survival felt less like resilience and more like endurance, an endless stretch of days where I moved forward because there was no other choice.

The emptiness and numbness were their own kind of torment. It left me suspended between feeling too much and feeling nothing at all, as if my heart couldn't decide whether to break open or shut down completely. I longed for comfort, for someone to step into the silence and remind me I was not alone; I was not motherless. I wanted a hand on my shoulder, a voice steady enough to anchor me, a presence strong enough to hold the weight I suddenly couldn't carry. But comfort never arrived.

Instead, there was only the echo of my own thoughts, questions that spiralled, memories that stung, and the quiet disbelief that someone so central to my existence could simply be gone. I kept waiting for the world to pause, to acknowledge the enormity of what had happened, but everything carried on with cruel normality. People walked, cars passed, conversations continued, and I stood there feeling like a shadow of myself. The numbness wasn't relief; it was a shield my mind threw up because the full truth was too heavy to face all at once.

In that strange, suspended space, I realised grief doesn't always announce itself with tears or wailing. Sometimes it arrives as a hollow ache, a quiet implosion, a sense that something essential has been removed from the architecture of your life. And in that void, you wait, hoping that someone, anyone, will notice the collapse and reach in to steady you. But when no one does, you're left to confront the silence on your own, learning slowly, painfully, how to breathe again in a world that feels permanently altered.

Grief, I have read, does not end. It reshapes how you live, breathe, and see the world. It settles into the spaces you once filled with certainty and rearranges the furniture of your inner life without asking permission. When my world stopped again, I realised survival is not about finding joy; it's about learning to exist in silence, carrying storms within, and hoping that one day the weight will feel less unbearable. After the loss of my mother, grief became a kind of second language, this constant negotiation between what was and what is.

I learnt to move through days with an ache that doesn't announce itself loudly but sits quietly beneath everything, colouring even the simplest moments. I also learnt to smile as something inside me trembled, while a part of me remained in the moment of loss, unable to step forward. And yet, in that strange, altered landscape, I also began to understand that survival is not a single act but a series of small, stubborn choices. Waking up. Getting dressed. Answering a message. I began to allow myself to breathe through the heaviness instead of fighting it. As this happened, I noticed that we don't heal in a dramatic burst; that when it comes in slow, uneven steps, when we begin to trust again, sometimes blindly, that the sharpest edges of grief will soften with time.

I also learnt that in grief, one doesn't wait for joy to return. That I simply have to hope that one day, the silence will feel less threatening, the storms inside will quieten, and the weight I carry will shift from something that crushes me to something I can live alongside. And in that hope, fragile as it is, one finds the faintest outline of a path forward.

And yet, amidst that darkness, something unexpected began to stir, not hope, not yet, but a strange awareness that life was still moving. The sun still rose, even when I did not want it to. The seasons still changed, even when I wished time would stop. Birds still traced their familiar paths across the sky, neighbours still swept their doorsteps, and the world continued its quiet routines as if gently insisting that I, too, must keep going. I did not know then, but those rhythms, the ordinary persistence of life, would become the first threads of grace weaving through my grief.

It wasn't dramatic or comforting in any obvious way. It was subtle, almost shy, arriving in small moments I barely noticed at first. A warm patch of sunlight on a cold morning. The sound of rain tapping against the window. A stranger holding a door open. These tiny, unremarkable gestures reminded me that the world had not closed in on itself, even if I had. They didn't erase the pain, but they softened its edges, offering brief pauses in the heaviness.

Slowly, without my permission or awareness, those moments began to accumulate. They formed a quiet counterweight to the sorrow I carried. I found myself breathing a little deeper, standing a little steadier, recognising that grief and grace can coexist, that one does not cancel the other. And in that fragile coexistence, I began, unknowingly, to journey toward something gentler. Not healing, not yet, but the faintest sense that healing might one day be possible.

After the Last Amen

When the house grew quiet, our voices kept us whole.

The days after the funeral unfolded slowly, as though time itself had become cautious. The world outside continued with its usual rhythm, cars passing, neighbours chatting, the sun rising with its familiar indifference, but inside the family, everything felt suspended. The air carried a heaviness that settled into the walls, the furniture, and the spaces where laughter once lived.

The house, once full of movement and noise, now felt too large. Every room held a memory. Every corner carried an echo. And each morning began with the same quiet question: How do we do today? There was no clear answer. Some days brought a fragile steadiness, while others felt like walking through fog, each step uncertain.

In those early days, the living room became the family's refuge, a place where we drifted without planning to, drawn by an unspoken need to be near one another. It was where we tried to piece ourselves together, even when the pieces didn't quite fit. One evening, as the sky dimmed into a soft blue-grey, we found ourselves gathered again. No one spoke at first. The silence wasn't uncomfortable; it was simply honest.

"I thought today would be easier," our youngest sibling finally said, staring at their hands. "But it wasn't. I woke up and… it just hit me again." And she burst into tears. My cousin nodded and spoke. "It's like that. You think you're okay, and then something small, a smell, a memory just pulls you right back." After which, she joined my younger sister, and they both sobbed.

A soft hum of agreement filled the room. Only it was a hum of tears and silent lamentations as we all joined them, and before we knew it, the whole house was in tears. Just as the sobbing was dying down, one of the younger voices chimed in.

"You know what helped me today? I watched that silly video Mum used to laugh at, the one with the goat screaming like a human. I laughed so hard I cried." A few chuckles rippled through the room. "Mum loved that ridiculous goat," someone added, shaking their head with a faint smile. "She'd replay it ten times and laugh harder each time."

The laughter faded into a gentle quiet, but the heaviness had lifted just a little. Another voice spoke, more hesitant. "I went for a walk this afternoon. I didn't plan to, but I just… needed air. I ended up talking out loud, like she was walking with me. It felt strange, but also comforting."

"That's not strange," someone replied warmly. "We all talk to her in our own ways. I did exactly that when I was cooking last evening. I remember telling her off for not being here to taste the food."

These small confessions, these glimpses into how each person was coping, became a kind of glue, holding us together when grief threatened to pull us apart. But not every moment was light. Sometimes, one person's sadness would spill over, and the whole room would feel it. One evening, my younger brother, my father's successor, broke down mid-sentence, unable to hold back the tears. "I'm sorry," he whispered. "I didn't mean to bring everyone down."

Immediately, my hand reached out to him. "You're not bringing anyone down. We're all carrying this. When one of us cries, it's not a burden, it's a reminder that we're human." Our eldest brother added softly, "We're allowed to fall apart. That's why we're here, to help each other stand again."

The room grew quiet, but this time the silence felt full, full of understanding, full of shared pain, full of grace. Eventually, the time came for everyone to return to their own destinations. Suitcases were packed, hugs were exchanged, and the house slowly emptied. The physical distance felt daunting. There was a quiet fear that once everyone scattered, the support might fade, and each person would be left alone with their grief.

But my family found a way to stay connected. Our WhatsApp forum, once used for jokes, updates, and everyday chatter, transformed into a lifeline. It became the new living room, the digital version of the family forum we had created in the house. Messages appeared at unexpected hours: "Rough morning today. Missing her a lot."

"I dreamt about her last night. Woke up crying but also grateful." Came the response. "Look what I found, her old photo from that trip to the UK to visit our brother and family.

Look at how lovely she looked, in trousers and a nice flowery top? It made me smile."

Sometimes the messages were long, pouring out thoughts too heavy to carry alone. Like the one from my younger brother to our elder brother detailing a past conversation about various medications, including blood pressure and temperature monitoring devices that we had bought to help monitor our parents' health. And how my siblings and I had done our utmost best to see to it that their medical needs were met, yet the cruel hand of death had another agenda. Other times, they were short, just a simple "Thinking of you all," but even those small words carried warmth.

There were voice notes too, shaky at times, steady at others, where someone would share a memory or talk about how they were coping. And whenever one person felt low, the others rallied around with words of comfort, humour, or simply presence.

"Take your time," someone would write.

"We're here."

"You're not alone."

The group became a space where grief could breathe. No one had to pretend. No one had to be strong all the time. And even though we were miles apart, the connection felt real, almost tangible. We shared memories, some tender, some hilarious, and each memory became a thread weaving us closer together. We shared coping strategies too: morning walks, journaling, listening to our parents' favourite songs, sharing their stories, or simply allowing ourselves to cry when the wave came.

In this digital space, we continued to cheer each other up, just as we had in the living room. We reminded one another that healing wasn't linear, that bad days didn't erase progress, and that grief didn't have to be carried alone. Over time, our group chats, late-night video calls, and shared playlists became a kind of virtual refuge. When one of us went quiet, another would send a voice note just to check in. When memories felt too heavy, we'd drop old photos into the chat, not to reopen wounds, but to honour the love that shaped us. Even though we were scattered in different places, technology let us recreate the closeness we once took for granted. It became our way of holding each other up, of stitching together a sense of family in the middle of loss, and of reminding ourselves that connection doesn't disappear just because the world has changed.

Drawing experience from Dad's passing, memories of which continue to linger with us years after, we already knew that the days after the funeral were not going to be easy. Despite that, we did not know they would be raw, disorienting, and often overwhelming. But losing him had quietly taught us things we didn't realise we'd need again – how grief can ambush you on an ordinary afternoon, how silence can feel heavier than words, and how important it is to reach for one another even when you don't know what to say. So, as we stuck together as a family, we discovered that grace could travel across distances. It could live in a message, a shared memory, a late-night voice note, or a simple "How are you holding up?" The lessons we learned from Dad's absence became the tools we leaned on after Mum's: to check in before someone asked, to listen without trying to fix, to make space for both laughter and tears. Strangely, the pain we had survived once before became a map, imperfect, but familiar enough to guide us back to each other when the world felt unbearably quiet.

As the clock ticked and the days passed, we were learning to breathe again, slowly, unevenly, but together. Grief hadn't loosened its grip, not yet. But through our continued support, our shared stories, and the willingness to show up for one another even from afar, healing had begun to take shape.

And in that shared journey across living rooms, cities, continents and screens, we found a new kind of strength. One shaped not by the absence of pain, but by the courage to face it side by side, even when separated by miles.

CHAPTER 8

Miles Between Me and Yesterday

The road did not judge me. It did not ask me to be strong. It
simply carried me forward, mile after mile.

The first long drive after Mum's burial was not merely a commute; it was a pilgrimage. The car became my sanctuary, a cocoon of steel and glass where grief could breathe freely. The first time I turned the key in the ignition for that long drive, I felt as though I was leaving behind more than a house; I was leaving behind a life. The road stretched out before me like an endless ribbon, and for the first time in months, I was alone with my thoughts. No condolences, no paperwork, no HR meetings, just me, the hum of the engine, and the ache that had become my constant companion.

The low rumble of the engine felt like a heartbeat steadying mine, gently urging me into motion when everything inside me wanted to stay still. The engine reluctantly stirred, its low hum filling the silence. I gripped the steering wheel, my knuckles whitening, as tears blurred the windscreen. The leather beneath my palms absorbed the tremors of grief, each sob sinking into the car's interior like invisible scars.

The tyres rolled forward, crunching over gravel before settling onto the smooth tarmac. The motorway stretched ahead, endless and unfeeling. Fields blurred into hedgerows, which blurred into towns; each landmark dissolved into the next. The rhythm of the journey was hypnotic: the ebb and flow of speed, the gentle sway of bends, the occasional bump of a pothole.

And then, within the rhythm of the drive, I imagined my mother's voice surfacing softly, imagined yet unmistakable. *"You're stronger than you think,"* Mum said, *as if she were sitting beside him.* I shook my head and whispered back, "I don't feel strong. I feel hollow." *"Hollow is not the same as broken,"* she replied. *"Hollow means there's room for something new to grow."*

The hum of the tyres became her lullaby, a soft, rhythmic whisper that seemed to rise from the road itself, carrying her words onwards long after she'd fallen silent. I pressed harder on the accelerator, not out of urgency, but out of a quiet, aching desire to stay wrapped in the comfort of her presence for just a little longer. The landscape blurred into muted streaks of colour as dusk settled, and the world felt suspended, just me, the road, and the echo of her voice threading through the cabin like a memory that refused to fade. Later, as the road wound through open fields and the horizon opened wide, I heard her again, faint but unmistakable, as though the wind had learned her cadence and was returning it to me piece by fragile piece.

"Don't be afraid of the unknown," she said. *"It's where life hides its surprises."* This thought made me whisper into the

wind, saying, *"I wish you were here to see it."* *"I am,"* she replied, her voice fading into the rush of air against the windows.

I did not expect the drive to feel so burdensome. Every mile carried the weight of memories, of my son's tiny fingers, my father's laughter, my mother's gentle wisdom, and the sense of purpose I once found in my work. They all accompanied me in the silence, like ghosts in the empty passenger seats. I gripped the steering wheel more tightly, as if holding on to something solid could prevent me from unravelling.

The steering wheel absorbed my sorrow as my hands gripped it tighter, knuckles pale this time, while tears blurred the horizon. Yet the road stretched ahead, indifferent and boundless, offering no judgment, only direction. The hum of the tyres on the road's surface continued the lullaby, soothing the ache in ways silence never could.

Solitude, once unbearable, began to feel like a strange comfort. With no one beside me, I could unravel freely, without masks, without forced strength. The car became a vessel for honesty, carrying both my brokenness and my hope. Inside those four doors, I could cry without apology, scream without judgment, and whisper prayers too fragile for the outside world. The rhythm of the tyres on the tarmac was strangely soothing, like a lullaby for a restless soul. I began to realise that movement was medicine; sometimes healing requires motion, even when you don't know where you're going. Each mile was a whispered prayer, a plea for healing carried into the wind. The rhythm of driving, accelerating, slowing, and turning mirrored the rhythm of grief: unpredictable yet always moving forward.

As the miles went by, the scenery began to take shape. Rolling hills, wide skies, and the way sunlight broke through the clouds felt like quiet sermons. Nature asked nothing of me; it simply existed, reminding me that life goes on even when hearts break. I started noticing small things, like how the fog lifted in the morning and how trees lined the road like silent guards. Each detail felt like a thread pulling me back towards hope.

As the landscape changed, fields gave way to towns, and towns melted into open stretches of road. I felt the symbolism grow stronger. I was leaving behind the life I knew, the one tied to Mum's presence, and moving towards the unknown. The destination was a new job, but the journey meant more: a passage into the next chapter of my life. The road became a bridge connecting yesterday and tomorrow.

By the time I reached the city's outskirts, the tears had dried, replaced by a quiet resolve. The car had carried me through the storm of my emotions, teaching me that healing does not always happen in stillness. Sometimes it occurs in motion, in the steady hum of tyres, in the endless stretch of road, in the act of simply carrying on.

There was something almost medicinal about the rhythm of the journey, the way the landscape shifted, the way the sky slowly opened, the way the world outside refused to pause even though my own heart felt suspended. With every mile, the weight inside me rearranged itself, not disappearing, but settling into a place where I could hold it without breaking.

Grief had entered the car with me, raw and overwhelming, but somewhere along that road, it softened, becoming less of a wave crashing over me and more of a tide I could learn to move with. The road didn't offer answers, but it offered space, space to breathe, to think, to feel without being consumed. And in that space, I found the first fragile threads of acceptance beginning to form.

Traffic thickened as I approached the city. Brake lights flashed, horns sounded, yet inside I felt lighter and steadier. The cocoon had done its work. The road had carried me through grief into possibility. I pulled into the parking lot of the new workplace, the building looming with unfamiliar promise. For a moment, I sat in the car, hands resting on the wheel, listening to the engine's fading hum.

In that small pocket of stillness, I felt the weight of everything I had travelled through settle behind me, not gone, but no longer pulling me under. The world outside was busy, indifferent, already moving on with its own rhythm, yet I felt strangely aligned with it, as though the journey had nudged me back into the current of my own life. The building ahead was unknown territory, a threshold into a future I had not yet imagined, but for the first time in a long while, the unknown didn't feel threatening. It felt open.

I took a slow breath, letting the air fill the space grief had hollowed out. My hands steadied on the wheel, not from certainty, but from a quiet acceptance that I was ready, ready to step out, ready to begin again, ready to carry her love forward into whatever waited beyond those doors.

Sitting there, I imagined hearing *"Go on, son,"* Mum's voice whispered. *"You've already taken the hardest step."* I nodded, exhaling slowly. The journey was not over; grief would return, as grief always does, but I had learnt something essential: the road did not require strength. It merely offered guidance. I stepped out and walked towards the doors, the air sharp against my face. Behind me lay miles of yesterday. Ahead, something unknown.

Looking back now, I realise that the drive was not merely about escape; it was about confrontation. With every mile, I faced the questions I had been avoiding: *Who am I now? What matters when everything familiar is gone?* The road did not provide answers, but it offered space, space to grieve, space to breathe, space to begin anew. That drive was more than a commute; it was the first step towards learning to live again.

By the time I reached my destination, something had shifted. The pain was still there, but it felt lighter, as if the road had absorbed some of it. I did not know then, but these drives would become my sanctuary, a moving chapel where grace would find me, mile after mile. There was a strange comfort in the way the world slipped past the windows, fields giving way to towns, towns dissolving into open stretches of sky. The motion itself seemed to loosen what grief had tightened inside me. With every turn of the wheels, something in me unclenched, making room for breath, for clarity, for the smallest flicker of hope.

In that quiet, enclosed space, I learned that healing doesn't always arrive with ceremony. Sometimes it comes in the form of a long road, a steady engine, and the simple act of continuing forward when standing still feels impossible. Those drives became the place where I could lay my sorrow down without fear, where the rhythm of the journey held me gently enough to let me feel and strong enough to keep me moving.

I didn't realise it then, but the road was teaching me how to live with loss, not by erasing it, but by carrying me far enough to see that even grief has its own horizon.

CHAPTER 9

The Road that Led Back to Her

*Some losses stay with us not because they broke us, but be-
cause they once held us so completely.*

The drive has taught me that grief is not a single moment but a long, winding road, bending, rising, and falling with the terrain of memory. Some losses sit quietly in the back seat, whispering only when the road grows still. Others ride in the passenger seat, insistent and unignorable, shaping every mile. And then there are those losses that take the wheel entirely, steering the journey long after the person is gone.

My loss of "Mami Nta'ambang, my mother's elder twin, my other mother in every sense that mattered," was one such loss. In the African way of family, where aunties and uncles are not linguistic categories but living extensions of one's parents, she was woven into the fabric of my upbringing. There was no "auntie" in our language. There was only 'mother,' expressed in different bodies, with different voices, but the same unbroken love. She was one of mine.

When she passed, I was in my early twenties, young enough to still be learning the shape of adulthood, yet old enough to feel the weight of responsibility pressing on my shoulders. I had just travelled to Europe, stumbling through the unfamiliar rhythms of a new world, trying to settle, trying to survive. And in the midst of that fragile beginning, news of her death reached me like a blow to the chest. I could not go home. I could not stand by her grave. I could not hold my mother as she mourned her twin, her other half. And so, the grief lodged itself inside me, unprocessed, unspoken, unresolved. It became a quiet passenger on my drive, one that refused to be left behind.

What made the pain sharper was not just the fact that she died, but the kind of woman she had been. She wasn't simply present in our lives; she was woven into them, a constant, steady, dependable force whose love showed itself not in grand gestures but in the quiet, instinctive ways she cared. She had a way of appearing exactly when she was needed most, as if she could sense trouble before anyone spoke it aloud. Her love for me was like that, unspoken, unwavering, and fierce in its loyalty.

I still remember the day my leg was broken in the field. I was young, frightened, and in pain, and the world felt suddenly too big and too cruel. Yet even in that moment, before I could fully understand what had happened, she was already moving toward me. My brother later told me how he had rushed home to raise the alarm, only to find her already there with my mother. Breathless from the journey, dust clinging stubbornly to her clothes, she had somehow heard of the accident and travelled nearly two hours across rough terrain to reach us. She didn't hesitate, didn't stop to rest, didn't think of herself. Her only thought, her only instinct was to get to me. That was her love: immediate, wholehearted, and without condition. She carried it like a torch, lighting the way for all of us, but especially for me, maybe because I was named after her father. And losing her meant losing not just an aunt, but one of the purest sources of love I have ever known.

"I don't know how she heard of it," my brother said, shaking his head even years later. "But she acted so fast. She was already home, waiting, wanting to know the next step." That was who she was, a 'mother in motion,' always moving toward those she loved. Her love did not hesitate. It did not calculate. It simply responded.

The Morning of 9/11 is another memory, this one not mine but my brother's, which has stayed with me like a carved stone. It was the morning of 9/11, the very day I was meant to board a London-bound flight from Douala. The world was unravelling in flames and confusion, and communication was scarce. Cell phones were not common, and news travelled in fragments, often distorted by fear. My brother recalls waking up early to find her already in our house.

"You had just left home," he told me. "And when we woke up, she was there. She had travelled down before dawn. After she heard about the attack, she couldn't rest. She had to come and make sure you were not affected." It was so like her, this instinctive, almost urgent need to protect me, as though my well-being were tied to her own heartbeat. She didn't wait for confirmation, didn't pause to gather herself, didn't even consider the darkness or the long road ahead. The moment she heard there might be danger near me, something in her spirit ignited. She rose before the sun, stepped into the cold morning air, and made her way to us with a determination that only love could fuel.

My brother said she looked exhausted when she arrived, her eyes shadowed from lack of sleep, her clothes still carrying the chill of the early morning. But the moment she heard that I was safe, something in her softened, relief washing over her so visibly it was as if she had been holding her breath for hours. That was the depth of her care: she carried my fears as if they were her own, and she never hesitated to cross any distance, physical or emotional, to reach me. That was the depth of Mami Nta'ambang's love, restless, protective, instinctive. She moved with the urgency of a mother whose child might be in danger. She did not wait for confirmation. She did not wait for clarity. She simply came.

To lose such a woman, such a mother, so early, and from so far away, carved a wound that time alone could not heal. It wasn't just grief, it was a tearing away, a sudden silence where a steady, loving presence had always been. It left an ache which I have come to realise is "The Ache of Unfinished Love." I carried that ache like a stone in my pocket, always there, always pressing against me, its weight shifting but never disappearing. What lingered most painfully was the sense of unfinished love, the conversations we never had, the gratitude I never fully expressed, the moments of care she would have offered if life had allowed her more time. There were so many ways she still would have shown up for me, so many instinctive acts of love she never got the chance to perform. And I, in turn, had so much more growing to do under her watchful eye, so many more chances to honour her, to reassure her that her sacrifices had shaped me.

It is a strange kind of sorrow, this unfinished love. It doesn't rage or shout; it settles quietly into the corners of your life, reminding you of what was beautiful and what was abruptly cut short. It is the ache of a bond interrupted mid-sentence, a love that had more to give, more to teach, more to become. She had poured so much into me, care, protection, and sacrifice, and I never had the chance to return even a fraction of it. I never got to stand by her bedside. I never got to say goodbye. I never got to honour her in person as she was laid to rest.

And so, the grief became a long drive with no clear destination. Some days the road was smooth, and I could almost convince myself that the ache had softened. Other days, a memory, a scent, a story, a familiar phrase would rise like a sudden bend in the road, and I would feel the loss all over again. But the drive has also taught me something else: grace often appears in the rear-view mirror. It comes quietly, in reflections, in the stories others tell, in the realisation that love does not end simply because a life has ended.

My brother's memories became a kind of grace for me, reminders of who she was, reminders that her love had been witnessed, felt, and remembered by many. Her legacy was not lost. It lived in the people she touched, in the journeys she made, in the sacrifices she offered without hesitation. And slowly, I began to understand that healing does not mean forgetting. It means learning to carry the memory differently, less like a burden and more like a compass.

Now, when I think of her, I imagine her on the drive with me, not as a ghost of grief, but as a quiet source of strength. I imagine her urging me forward, reminding me that love is not measured by the chance to repay it, but by the fact that it was given freely. Her life was a testament to that truth. Her love was a road that always led home. And though she left too soon, though I never got to say goodbye, though the ache still rises on certain bends of the journey, I carry her with me, not as a wound, but as a guiding presence, one that reminds me that grace is found not only in healing, but in remembering.

CHAPTER 10

Landscapes of Healing

Healing did not come in grand gestures; it came in the way the morning light touched the horizon.

Healing did not arrive all at once. It came in fragments, small, almost unnoticed shifts that began during the journey. At first, the drive was merely a necessity, a way to get to a job that paid less than I had hoped. But as the miles went on, something unexpected happened: the world outside my window started to speak.

The land started to speak in ways I had not noticed before. Rolling hills stretched out like a gentle hymn, their curves steady and unhurried, teaching me that progress does not always announce itself; it often arrives silently, in the soft rise and fall of the earth beneath your feet. Each hill carried me upwards into a new perspective, then downwards into rest, reminding me that both effort and pause are parts of the same journey.

The mornings told their own stories. One morning, I woke before the world appeared awake. The air was cool, carrying the faint scent of damp earth. As I walked along a narrow path between fields towards my car, the horizon began to soften. The first light spread across the hills, gilding them with pale gold. It was not dramatic; it was gentle, like a hand resting softly on my shoulder. In that quiet hour, I felt the weight inside me lift. The sunrise was not a spectacle to admire from afar; it was a promise whispered directly to me: You will not stay in darkness forever.

On another morning, the fog was so thick it felt like driving through grief itself, dense, suffocating, and impossible to see beyond. The world shrank to the small circle of visibility ahead of my headlights, and every metre felt like a step taken in faith rather than certainty. Yet, gradually, the mist lifted, and sunlight spread across the hills like grace breaking through despair. That image stayed with me. It was as if nature were giving a quiet sermon: *This, too, will clear. This too will pass.*

There was something profoundly comforting in that slow unveiling of the world, the way the light didn't rush or force itself but arrived gently, as though mindful of the weight I carried. It reminded me that healing often comes in the same way, not in sudden revelations, but in soft, steady brightness that returns piece by piece. The fog had felt endless while I was inside it, just as grief often does, but the moment it thinned, I realised it had been moving all along.

That morning taught me that even when life feels obscured, when the path ahead is blurred by sorrow or fear, clarity has a way of finding us. Sometimes all we can do is keep moving, trusting that the light will meet us somewhere along the road.

The landscapes became my companions. Rolling fields, winding roads, and skies painted in shades of orange and violet reflected my inner journey. On days when my heart felt heavy, the clouds seemed to gather in solidarity. On days when hope flickered, the sun broke through like a promise. I started to notice details I had previously ignored, such as the way trees stood like sentinels, the rhythm of rivers flowing effortlessly, and the resilience of wildflowers blooming in harsh soil.

Each scene delivers a lesson. The hills showed me that life has gradients; some climbs are steep, but they lead to landscapes worth seeing. The rivers reminded me that movement is vital, even when the path twists and turns. The wildflowers whispered that beauty could flourish in broken places. These were not just landscapes; they served as metaphors for survival, resilience, and grace.

The more I travelled, the more I realised that the world around me was quietly instructive. The wind sweeping across open fields taught me that change is constant, and resisting it only exhausts the soul. The shifting clouds overhead reminded me that emotions, like weather, are allowed to move, to darken, to clear. Even the distant mountains, silent, immovable, seemed to speak of endurance, of the strength found in simply standing through the seasons.

Every mile offered a new parable, a reminder that healing is stitched together from small revelations. Nature became a patient teacher, showing me that life continues to grow, bend, and bloom despite storms. And in those lessons, I found a language for my own survival, a way to understand that grief and grace often walk the same path.

The skies also became storytellers. I watched them transform from heavy grey to sudden flashes of colour, as if grief and joy were painted on the same canvas. Storm clouds gathered like old sorrows, pressing close, but they never stayed. They broke apart, dissolved, and made way for light. And when dawn arrived, spilling gold across the horizon, it felt less like a spectacle and more like a promise whispered directly to me: you will not remain in darkness forever.

There were mornings when fog wrapped around the road, obscuring everything familiar. Driving through it felt like moving inside uncertainty, with each turn hidden until I came upon it. My hands tightened on the wheel, my breath shallow, as though the mist outside reflected the confusion within me. Yet, mile by mile, the fog began to lift. Trees emerged, their shadows becoming sharper, and the road stretched clear once more. Just as mist lifts from the fields, clarity started to return within me. The fog in my chest, the heaviness, and the confusion gradually thinned until I could see the path ahead again.

Nature spoke in that moment: it whispered that healing is not sudden, but gradual, like mist unravelling thread by thread. I realised then that clarity does not arrive all at once; it comes gradually, like mist unravelling thread by thread. The landscape taught me patience: healing is not sudden, but slow, and it asks us to trust the unseen path.

Another day, I found myself standing by the window as the day folded into evening. The sky was painted in layers of lavender, rose, and deepening indigo. Shadows stretched long across the valley and then softened into the embrace of night. I sat there, watching the sun sink, and felt a quiet release. The end of the day was not sorrowful; it was graceful, reminding me that even endings contain beauty. The ordinary act of watching the sky change became extraordinary when I allowed myself to notice. Hope arrived not as thunder but as stillness.

It arrived quietly, not through grand gestures. It was in the way dew caught the first light, transforming blades of grass into jewelled strands. It was in the way a bird's song pierced silence with simple joy. It was in the way shadows stretched long and then retreated, reminding me that even endings hold beauty. Ordinary scenery became extraordinary when I allowed myself to notice. Its grace was quiet, but it was enough.

Walking through these landscapes, I began to realise that healing is not a goal but a rhythm. The hills, the skies, the fog, and the light reflected the shifts within me. Where once I saw only barrenness, I started to see renewal. Where once I felt only endings, I began to sense new beginnings. Nature spoke, not in words but through presence. And I listened.

With each step, I felt myself syncing to something older and wiser than my grief. The earth beneath my feet seemed to pulse with its own steady heartbeat, reminding me that life continues even when we feel paused. The wind carried whispers of change, brushing against me with a gentleness that felt like reassurance. Even the silence had a texture to it, thick, patient, and strangely comforting, as if the world was holding space for me to breathe again.

Slowly, I began to understand that healing wasn't something I had to chase or force. It unfolded in its own time, the way dawn unfolds across a dark horizon. The landscapes didn't demand anything from me; they simply existed, steady and unhurried, inviting me to do the same. And in that quiet companionship, I found myself softening, opening, learning to trust that life still had room for beauty, for growth, for me.

I started pulling over at service stations or by the roadside, sometimes not because I needed a break but because I needed to breathe in the beauty. I would stand by the roadside, watching the horizon stretch endlessly, and feel something loosen inside me. The grief was still there, but it was no longer choking me. It was becoming part of the scenery, a shadow that existed alongside the light.

Healing, I realised, does not always happen within hospitals or therapy rooms. Sometimes, it occurs on a quiet road, beneath an open sky, with only the hum of an engine and the whisper of wind through the trees. The landscapes did not erase my pain, but they reframed it. They reminded me that life, like the road, keeps moving, and so could I.

CHAPTER 11

Conversations with the Road

Every mile speaks. In the quiet hum of the tyres and the endless stretch of tarmac, the road becomes a companion, listening, guiding, and reminding us that healing often happens between destinations.

The road became my personal confessional. Not the kind lined with wooden panels, dim light, and whispered prayers, where a priest sits in for Jesus and waits for you to spill your sins, but the long, unbroken ribbon of asphalt that absorbs everything without judgment. Out there, with nothing but the hum of the engine and the steady rhythm of passing lines, the world finally quiets down enough for the truth to speak up.

When I drive, questions rise like ghosts in the rearview mirror, persistent, uninvited, impossible to ignore. They drift in and settle beside me, asking things I spend the rest of my life trying not to hear. *Questions like: What am I actually doing with my life? Where does faith go when doubt starts shouting louder than hope? Why does meaning slip through my fingers just when I'm sure I've finally caught hold of it?*

The road doesn't answer, of course. It just listens. And somehow, that's enough to keep me driving a little farther, as if the next mile might finally offer clarity, or at least a moment where the questions feel a little less heavy. I speak to them aloud sometimes, half-hoping the steering wheel will respond. It never does. Instead, the rhythm of tyres against the pavement becomes a kind of reassurance, a steady heartbeat reminding me that movement itself is enough.

I remember a particular Monday morning when I had just set off at 4 am to undertake the four-hour-plus journey to my office at the other end of the country. The rain had just started, soft at first, then steady enough to drum against the windscreen. The smell of wet earth seeped through the vents, mingling with the faint scent of coffee still lingering in the cup holder. My hands rested on the steering wheel, cool and firm beneath my palms, as the headlights carved tunnels of light through the blur of passing drops.

I spoke into the quiet. *"Why does it feel like I'm forever chasing something I can't quite name?"* The words floated into the cabin of the car, fragile and half-formed, as if saying them aloud might make them dissolve. The road responded in its own way, not with answers but with presence, long, unbroken stretches of tarmac unfolding like a patient companion. The hum of the tyres softened into something almost human, a low, steady voice murmuring, *"Keep going."*

Out there, in that strange sanctuary of motion and solitude, it felt as though the world had stepped back just enough for me to hear myself think. The sky stretched wide and indifferent above me, the horizon refusing to hurry, and I found a strange comfort in that. Maybe the road didn't know where I was headed either, but it was willing to take me there anyway. And somehow, that felt like enough for the moment, a quiet permission to keep searching, even if I didn't yet know what for.

I laughed softly, shaking my head. *"You're not much of a therapist, you know."* My voice sounded small in the cabin, swallowed almost instantly by the steady drone of the engine. *"You don't give answers. Do you?"* It felt like an accusation and a confession at the same time.

But the road, in its quiet, stubborn way, seemed to whisper back, not with words but with presence. *"Maybe you don't need answers. Maybe you just need space."* The thought drifted through me like a breeze through an open window, gentle, unexpected, unsettling in its truth. The miles stretched out ahead, wide and indifferent, offering nothing but room to breathe. And maybe that was the point. Maybe the road wasn't there to fix me or guide me or hand me some neatly packaged revelation. Maybe it was simply holding the silence long enough for me to hear the things I'd been drowning out. The things I wasn't brave enough to face when the world was too close and too loud.

So I kept driving, letting the asphalt do what it did best, carry me forward, even when I wasn't sure where forward was. The road became more than just a path; it became a confidant. In the quiet hum of the engine and the steady rhythm of tyres on asphalt, I found a space where my thoughts could finally breathe. At first, the silence was intimidating. It felt like stepping into a vast, empty room where grief echoed louder than ever, bouncing off invisible walls until it filled every corner of me. But over time, that silence transformed into something sacred, a sanctuary for conversations I couldn't have anywhere else.

I spoke to the road as if it could hear me. As if the dark ribbon of asphalt had some ancient wisdom tucked beneath its surface. I asked questions that had no answers, the kind that sit heavy in the chest long before they ever reach the tongue. "*Why them? Why now? Why me?*" The words felt too small for the weight they carried, dissolving into the air the moment they left my mouth. The road didn't flinch. It didn't offer comfort or clarity. It just kept stretching forward, mile after mile, as if to say that some questions aren't meant to be solved, they're meant to be survived. And in that strange, quiet way, the road held space for the grief, the confusion, the rawness of not knowing. It let me pour it all out without demanding that I make sense of any of it.

I confessed fears I had not admitted even to myself, the fear of being forgotten, the fear of never finding joy again, the fear that I was somehow broken beyond repair. Even the fear of not knowing what will happen to my family or me when I am no more. Though the road never spoke back, it listened. It absorbed my words without judgment, without interruption, without the hollow reassurances people often give when they don't know what to say.

Each mood on the road became a distinct voice, shaping the conversation. For example, in the brightness of some mornings, the road felt like a gentle teacher. On these occasions, the sun warmed the dashboard, and the air rushing through the open window smelled of grass and dust. Following that, the road whispers, "Look ahead. See how far you can go."

Even music on such daylight mornings seemed lighter, playful even. Each note reminded me that joy is not gone; it's waiting to be noticed. Even the road's voice in these hours was steady and encouraging, nudging me towards hope, reminding me that clarity often arrives when shadows are shortest.

As I drove on, deep in thought, the dashboard lights glowed faintly in the dark, casting shadows across my hands. The steering wheel felt cool beneath my grip, grounding me when my thoughts threatened to spiral. Outside, headlights stretched across the pavement like brushstrokes of gold, and the blur of passing trees became a rhythm, a heartbeat that matched my own.

Similarly, the road whispered during night drives. When darkness envelops the car, I notice that the road's voice shifts. Headlights carve tunnels through the blackness, and the hum of the tyres becomes a soft, intimate murmur. During these moments, I seemed to hear the road whisper: "This is the time for honesty. Speak the things you hide in daylight."

Even during rainy and stormy drives, when rain lashes against the windscreen and thunder rolls in the distance, I imagined the road's voice growing louder, almost defiant. The wipers struggle, the world blurs, and the smell of rain fills the car. The road shouts, "Let it out. Don't hold back. The storm is big enough to carry your grief."

At this moment, I noticed that music during storms became raw and urgent. For some reason, I started singing along, voice cracking, tears mixing with laughter. The road, slick but unwavering, taught me that chaos can be cleansing. Its voice in these moments is fierce yet freeing, reminding me that relief often comes amid turmoil. What is also interesting is that I noticed songs at night carried weight. Certain songs and slow refrains, such as Blessed Assurance, stirred memories I thought I had buried. In the night, the road listens like a confidant of secrets, holding my doubts without judgment. Its silence was not empty; it became an invitation to face what I fear most.

Music became my second companion. Some songs cracked me open, pulling tears from places I thought had dried up. Others stitched me together, note by note, reminding me that beauty still existed even in the midst of sorrow. I built playlists, including my late parents' favourite songs and the tribute song dedicated to my late mother. I had songs for mornings when getting out of bed felt impossible, songs for evenings when loneliness pressed against the windows like fog. Each melody carried a memory, and each memory carried a lesson.

However, the most profound conversations occurred in the pauses between songs, in the silence that followed. That silence was not empty; it was filled with whispers I had been too busy to notice. Whispers of resilience, whispers of grace, whispers of a voice I had lost in the chaos, my own voice, my own reflective imagination. In those moments, I realised that healing does not always come through answers; sometimes it comes from listening to the questions without rushing to find solutions.

The road taught me something essential: movement does not remove pain, but it gives pain a rhythm. It transforms grief from a stagnant pool into a flowing river, carrying it forward mile after mile until it feels lighter, even if only for a short while. In that rhythm, I began to rediscover a truth I had forgotten, that life, like the road, keeps going. And so, I could too.

CHAPTER 12

Grace in the Rearview Mirror

Grace did not come with trumpets; it came like a whisper, re-minding me that I was not alone.

Grace is often misunderstood as something dramatic, a divine rescue that sweeps us off our feet. Yet more often, it arrives quietly, woven into the ordinary rhythms of life. My graces did not arrive with fanfare. They did not come in grand gestures or dramatic breakthroughs. Instead, they came quietly, as a whisper on the wind, showing up in moments so ordinary I almost missed them.

For months, I had been driving with my eyes fixed on the horizon, searching for something, peace, purpose, maybe even myself. Every mile felt like a question I couldn't quite articulate, every sunrise a reminder that I still hadn't found what I was chasing. But one day, almost by accident, I glanced in the rear-view mirror and realised grace had been riding with me all along. It hadn't arrived with trumpets or some cinematic breakthrough. It hadn't demanded I stop the car and pay attention. Instead, it had travelled quietly beside me, patient and unassuming.

Grace doesn't stride in with fanfare or insist on being acknowledged. It doesn't need to. It slips into the unnoticed corners of our days, the small, easily overlooked moments that don't feel holy until much later. It shows up in the stranger who holds a door a second longer than necessary, in the colleague who asks how you're really doing, in the unexpected kindness that feels almost too ordinary to be divine. And yet, somehow, it is. Grace hides in the mundane, waiting for the moment we finally turn our heads and see it sitting there, steady and familiar, as if it had never left.

For me, it began with small acts of kindness. Nothing dramatic, nothing that would make a headline, just the gentle, almost invisible gestures that soften the edges of a hard day. At the petrol station, it was the attendant's smile, simple and unremarkable, yet warm enough to loosen something tight in my chest. I hadn't realised how long I'd been bracing myself against the world until that moment of uncomplicated friendliness met me where I stood.

In the office, it was a colleague's quiet encouragement, offered without fanfare or expectation. A few sincere words, a nod that said I see you, and suddenly the doubts that had been gnawing at me felt a little less convincing. It reminded me that my efforts mattered, even when my own mind insisted they didn't.

And then, in a moment of laughter shared with friends, one of those unplanned, unpolished bursts of joy, grace broke through like sunlight piercing a heavy sky. It didn't erase the struggle or pretend it wasn't there. Instead, it illuminated the truth that joy and sorrow aren't opposites at all. They coexist, weaving through each other, reminding us that even in seasons of heaviness, light still finds a way in.

Those small moments didn't fix everything. But they shifted something. They whispered that grace doesn't always arrive with grandeur; sometimes it comes disguised as the ordinary, waiting patiently for us to notice.

At home, it was my wife, always watching, always noticing the things I tried to hide. She would pause in the hallway, tilt her head slightly, and ask, *"Are you OK?"* in that gentle way of hers that made the question feel less like an interrogation and more like an invitation. When I opened the door after a long drive, shoulders slumped and eyes tired, she would quietly reach for my bag before I could protest, as if to say, *"Let me carry a little of this with you."* Her kindness didn't arrive with speeches or solutions; it lived in the small, steady gestures that reminded me I wasn't walking through life alone.

Then there was my son, who had somehow mastered the art of checking in without making it obvious. A text pinging through with the football results, or a quick call to tell me who scored and how the match ended, little things, but chosen with care. He knew I loved the game, and he knew that sometimes distraction is its own kind of medicine. His updates were his way of saying, *"I'm thinking of you,"* even if he never said the words outright.

And on other days, grace came through our gentle Prof, as we nicknamed him. Though autistic and nonverbal, he had a way of communicating that bypassed language entirely. He would stand in front of me, studying my face with a seriousness that felt almost sacred, then offer a soft, deliberate, *"You have got this."* The words were few, but the conviction behind them was unmistakable. Other times, he didn't speak at all. He would simply sit beside me, his hand resting on my arm, grounding me with a presence that said more clearly than any sentence, "*I am here with you.*" In those moments, his quiet companionship felt like a kind of grace I hadn't known how to name.

These were the places where grace lived, in the familiar walls of home, in the people who loved me without needing explanations, in the small gestures that stitched me back together when I didn't realise I was coming undone. Sometimes it was a song on the radio that played at just the right moment, reminding me that beauty still existed in a world that felt broken. These were not coincidences; they were threads of grace weaving through the fabric of my days.

I began to see grace in the ordinary rhythms of life. Not in grand revelations or dramatic turning points, but in the steady, faithful patterns that had been unfolding around me long before I ever thought to pay attention. In the way the sun rose each morning, unhurried, unwavering, casting light across the world even when my own heart felt unbearably heavy. Its consistency became a kind of reassurance, a reminder that some things remain steady even when I don't.

I saw it in the laughter of a child at a roadside café, a bright, unfiltered sound that cut straight through the fog of my thoughts. For a moment, it was as if the world cracked open just enough for joy to slip through, like sunlight breaking through a stubborn bank of clouds. That small burst of laughter didn't fix anything, but it reminded me that beauty still existed, even in the midst of my grief.

And then there were the wildflowers, those stubborn, resilient bursts of colour blooming along the motorway. They had no business thriving in such harsh soil, battered by wind and ignored by everyone rushing past. Yet there they were, defiantly alive. Their quiet resilience felt like a message I hadn't realised I needed: life persists, even in unlikely places. Grace was everywhere, woven into the fabric of the everyday, as it had always been. But grief had narrowed my vision, blinding me to the gentle mercies scattered throughout my days. It wasn't that grace had been absent; it was that I had forgotten how to see it.

The rear-view mirror became a metaphor for reflection. Looking back, I saw not only loss but also survival. I saw the miles I had travelled, the storms I had endured, and the strength I had not known I possessed. Grace was not about erasing pain; it was about giving me the courage to carry it without being crushed. It was about reminding me that even in the darkest seasons, light finds a way to seep through the cracks.

I realised then that grace is not earned; it's received. It's not a reward for resilience; it's a gift for the broken. And sometimes it shows up in the simplest ways: a kind word, a quiet moment, a breath of peace on a long drive. Grace does not always change our circumstances, but it changes us, and that is enough.

As I drove on, I stopped searching for grace on the horizon. I knew where to find it now, in the rear-view mirror, in the present moment, and in the quiet assurance that I was not alone on this road.

Looking back, I can say I have seen grace in the rear-view mirror not as a single event but as a series of divine whispers. Each kindness, each encouragement, each moment of joy is evidence of God's hand at work. Grace reminds us that we are never abandoned, never left to walk alone.

73

CHAPTER 13

Redefining Success in My World

I thought I had lost everything. But in losing, I found what mattered most.

For most of my life, success had a clear definition: a good job, a steady pay slip, and maybe, just maybe, a title such as Manager, Team Leader, or even Director that carried weight. I was almost convinced that the higher the salary, the greater the validation. I chased success like oxygen, convinced that climbing the corporate ladder was the only way to prove my worth. But the higher I climbed, the heavier the burden grew. Weekends blurred into weekdays, family dinners became rare, and my dreams outside work were shelved in the name of ambition.

It was the rhythm I lived by, the promotions, the performance reviews, the steady climb that made me feel competent, valued, indispensable. I measured my worth in deadlines met, problems solved, and the subtle thrill of being the person others relied on. Achievement became its own kind of heartbeat, a rhythm I didn't question because it kept me moving, kept me feeling alive.

But grief has a way of dismantling illusions with a single, brutal sweep. When I lost my parents and then my job, the scaffolding of my identity collapsed in on itself. All the structures I had leaned on, career, competence, the illusion of control, buckled under the weight of loss. Suddenly, the things I thought mattered most felt hollow, like props on a stage after the audience has gone home. The titles, the praise, the sense of being needed… none of it could anchor me anymore.

In the quiet that followed, I realised how much of myself I had poured into roles that could vanish overnight. I had built my life around being productive, useful and strong. But grief stripped all of that away, leaving me face-to-face with a version of myself I barely recognised, one who wasn't sure what remained when the doing stopped, and only the being was left.

When I walked away from my higher-paying job, I felt as though I was betraying everything I had worked for. It wasn't just a career shift; it felt like a dismantling of the story I had spent years telling myself. The titles, the promotions, the salary, all of it had become more than milestones; they had become my identity. I had woven my worth into the size of my payslip and the prestige of my role, convincing myself that success was something you could measure in numbers and accolades.

So taking a lower-paying job was not part of the plan. It felt like stepping backwards, like admitting defeat in a race I had been running for so long I no longer remembered why I started. I worried about what people would think, how they would interpret the shift, would they see it as failure, or worse, as proof that I had somehow squandered the opportunities I'd been given?

But beneath all that fear was something quieter, something I had ignored for years: the realisation that the life I had built was no longer sustainable. The pace, the pressure, the constant need to prove myself, it had all become too heavy to carry. Walking away wasn't a betrayal. It was an act of survival. Yet at the time, all I could feel was the sting of letting go of the version of myself I had worked so hard to maintain.

It felt like failure at first, a demotion not only in salary but in status. I remember staring at my first payslip, the numbers glaring back at me like a verdict: *You've fallen.* It was astonishing how quickly shame found its way in, whispering that I had lost not only my parents and my career but also my worth. It told me I had slipped from who I was supposed to be, that I had somehow let life outpace me. For weeks, I carried that weight like a stone lodged in my chest, heavy and immovable, wondering whether I would ever feel whole again.

At first, none of it made sense. I mourned the loss of the life I had built, the structure, the certainty, the identity that came with being "successful." I worried endlessly about what people would think. Would they see me as someone who couldn't keep up anymore, someone who had been overtaken by circumstances? Would they whisper that I had settled for less, that I had squandered the trajectory I once seemed destined for?

Those thoughts clung to me like fog, distorting everything I saw. But as the days passed and the miles stretched out beneath my tyres, the road began to teach me something different. It didn't lecture or correct me. It simply held space, mile after mile of quiet, steady presence. And in that stillness, I began to realise that maybe what I had lost wasn't worth clinging to in the first place. Maybe the version of success I had been chasing had never truly belonged to me. Maybe stepping down wasn't falling; it was finally stepping out of a life that had grown too small.

The road didn't give me answers, but it gave me room to breathe. And in that breathing space, the shame slowly loosened its grip, making way for something gentler, something truer.

Each long drive gave me space to question the old definitions of success. Out there, with nothing but the open road and the steady hum of the engine, the questions rose uninvited but necessary. *"Was it really about money or titles? Or was it about something deeper, peace, purpose, the ability to breathe without anxiety clawing at my throat?"* For the first time in years, I allowed myself to sit with those questions instead of outrunning them.

Slowly, almost imperceptibly, I began to see that success was not a destination; it was a state of being. It wasn't something I could earn, accumulate, or display. It was waking up without dread pressing against my ribs. It was feeling my shoulders loosen instead of tightening the moment I opened my eyes. It was finding joy in small mercies, the kind I had been too busy, too driven, too distracted to notice before.

On those drives, I had time to see the world again. I noticed the way sunlight danced on the dashboard, flickering like a quiet blessing. I noticed how the sky shifted from grey to gold without asking for applause. I noticed how my breath settled when I stopped trying to prove something and simply allowed myself to exist. The road didn't give me answers, but it gave me clarity: success wasn't out there somewhere. It was already within reach, woven into the ordinary moments I had been speeding past for years.

The new job, though modest, offered something priceless: simplicity. Fewer demands, less pressure, more room to heal. It gave me evenings to sit in silence without emails buzzing like angry bees. It gave me mornings to watch the sunrise without rushing to beat traffic. In losing what I thought was everything, I gained what I truly needed: space to rediscover myself. Space to grieve properly and share my thoughts on the healing process so they can become the grace others need.

Redefining success did not happen overnight. It was a slow, often painful unlearning of old narratives I had carried for years, stories about worth, achievement, and what it meant to live a meaningful life. Those beliefs had settled so deeply into me that letting them go felt like peeling away layers of skin. Some days, I clung to the familiar definitions out of habit; other days, I felt them slipping through my fingers no matter how tightly I tried to hold on.

But as the miles stretched behind me, something in me began to shift. The road, with its quiet patience, gave me room to breathe, to question, to unravel. And in that spaciousness, I realised that life is not measured in promotions or payslips; it's measured in peace. In grace. In the quiet assurance that you are enough, even when the world insists otherwise. It's measured in the mornings when you wake without dread pressing against your ribs, in the evenings when you can sit still without feeling the need to prove your worth to anyone, not even to yourself.

Slowly, I began to understand that success wasn't something external I had to chase. It was something internal I had to nurture. It lived in the small, steady moments of being present. It lived in the gentle acceptance of who I was becoming. And as I drove, watching the landscape shift and the sky open wide above me, I realised that perhaps I had been successful all along, I had just been looking in the wrong places. I did not merely accept the new definition of success; I embraced it. In doing so, I found freedom. Freedom from the tyranny of comparison, freedom from the relentless chase for more, and freedom to live a life that feels whole, even if it looks small.

I began to notice the little things: the joy of a slow morning, the freedom to pursue hobbies I had abandoned, and the warmth of friendships rekindled. I realised that the currency of life is not money; it's moments. And those moments, once lost to endless work, became my new measure of success.

I had spent years chasing titles, believing they defined me. But titles fade. What endures is meaning, found in the quiet, ordinary joys that make life rich. Looking back, I see that accepting a lower-paying job was not a punishment; it was a gift. A gift that allowed me to redefine success not as recognition from others but as fulfilment within myself.

Healing at 70 Miles an Hour

I did not just survive grief; I drove through it, and somewhere along the way, I began to live again.

The road became my companion when people felt too far away. When conversations felt too heavy or too hollow, the open stretch of motorway offered a kind of presence that didn't demand anything from me. At seventy miles an hour, I found a rhythm that matched the pulse of my healing, steady, unhurried, honest. The world blurred at the edges, and for the first time in a long while, I felt something inside me begin to loosen.

The steady hum of the tyres reminded me that life keeps moving forward, even when I felt stuck in place. Something was comforting in that mechanical constancy, as if the car itself was breathing for me on the days I forgot how. The white lines flicking past became a quiet metronome, marking time not by productivity or achievement but by simple existence. And slowly, mile by mile, I began to trust that I could move forward too. Not in leaps or dramatic breakthroughs, but in small, almost imperceptible shifts, the kind you only notice when you look back and realise the landscape has changed.

The road didn't heal me. But it held me. It carried me when I didn't know how to carry myself. And in that holding, I found the courage to believe that healing was possible, even if it came in fragments.

Healing did not announce itself with a trumpet blast. It crept in quietly, disguised as ordinary moments on the road. At first, I did not notice. I was too busy surviving, too busy gripping the steering wheel like a lifeline, too busy counting the miles between grief and obligation. But somewhere along the way, something shifted. The tears that once blurred my vision became less frequent. The silence that once felt suffocating began to feel like peace.

I remember the first time I laughed in the car after the loss. It was unplanned; it just happened. A song came on from my playlist, one I had not heard in years, and I found myself singing along with the driver's-side mirror down. Suddenly, I heard a passenger in the car next to me say, *"You are having a good time, aren't you?"* Not realising I was shaking my head along to the tune, I said, *"Yes, thank you!"*

I laughed at myself, at the sheer joy of being alive enough to sing again. That was a small grace I had not realised, and it took a stranger in a car travelling in the same direction to remind me. For months, I had been silent, carrying grief like a weight pressing down on my chest. That day, sound returned, and with it, a piece of me I thought was gone forever.

Joy slipped in unnoticed, like sunlight through a half-opened curtain. It didn't arrive with fanfare or sweep away the heaviness that had settled in my chest. Instead, it crept in softly, almost shyly, warming the cold corners of my heart before I even realised it was there. That moment did not erase the pain; grief still sat beside me, familiar and uninvited, but it reminded me that pain and joy can coexist, that they are not enemies but companions in the strange landscape of healing. It showed me that laughter can bloom in the soil of loss, fragile yet fiercely alive. A small smile, a shared joke, a fleeting moment of lightness, these were not betrayals of the people I had lost or the life I once knew. They were signs that my heart, though bruised, was still capable of opening. Joy didn't demand that I move on; it simply reminded me that I could move forward, carrying both sorrow and hope in the same pair of hands.

My grace and healing did not arrive in a single moment of clarity. There was no lightning bolt, no sudden revelation that stitched everything back together. It came in fragments, small, almost forgettable moments that only made sense when I looked back and realised they had been carrying me all along. It came in the soft glow of the dashboard during late-night drives, when the world felt hushed and forgiving, as if the darkness itself was permitting me to rest. In those quiet hours, the road wrapped around me like a blanket, and for a few miles at a time, the ache inside me loosened.

It came in the freedom of rolling down the windows and letting the wind rush in, cool and insistent, as though it were sweeping through the cluttered rooms of my heart. The wind didn't take the sorrow away, but it carried enough of it off my shoulders for me to breathe again. It came in the unexpected moments when I realised I could feel whole again, maybe not the same as before, maybe not without scars, but whole in a new way. A way that made room for both the pain that shaped me and the hope that refused to leave.

Healing didn't arrive as a single gift. It arrived as a collection of small mercies: a breath that didn't hurt, a night that didn't feel endless, a moment of stillness where I caught myself thinking, "*Maybe I'm going to be OK.*" And in those fragments, grace quietly rebuilt what grief had undone.

There were nights when I pulled over just to breathe, to sit in the stillness and remind myself that I was safe. Other nights, I kept driving, chasing the horizon, in the hope of not arriving back home too late, headlights stretching into the dark. Somewhere between mile markers, I realised I was not just surviving anymore, I was living.

Grace found me in unexpected places. At gas stations where strangers smiled. In the rhythm of windshield wipers during a storm. In the silence between songs, I could hear my own heartbeat. Healing was not waiting for me at the end of the road; it was happening in the middle of it, in the act of moving, of choosing to keep going even when I did not know where the road would lead.

Looking back now, I see the miles as chapters of recovery. Each stretch of highway taught me something: that joy can return in laughter, that wholeness can be felt in solitude, and that grace does not wait for us at the finish line; it meets us right where we are, even at seventy miles an hour.

The car itself became more than a machine. It was my sanctuary on wheels, a moving chapel where I could grieve, pray, sing, and be reborn. Its frame held my tears like stained glass holds light. Its windows opened to let in hope. Its engine hummed like a hymn, steady and faithful, reminding me I was still here. Every journey was less about the destination and more about the transformation. The car was my sacred space, a vessel that carried me from silence into song, from sorrow into laughter, from surviving into living.

The road taught me that healing is not a destination; it's a rhythm. It's the steady hum of tyres on the road surface, the way the horizon keeps moving even when you feel stuck. It's the realisation that grief does not vanish; it transforms. It becomes a companion rather than a captor, riding quietly in the backseat while you reclaim the driver's seat of your life.

I began to savour the drives. Not as escapes, but as sacred spaces. Each mile was a meditation, each turn a reminder that forward is possible. I learned to breathe deeply, to notice the way sunlight danced on the dashboard, to let gratitude seep in for things I once overlooked: the warmth of a cup of coffee, the kindness of a stranger, the resilience of my own heart.

Healing at 70 miles an hour did not mean forgetting. It meant integrating, carrying the love and the loss without letting them weigh me down. It meant finding grace in motion, hope in horizons, and strength in the simple act of moving forward.

As I look back into my rearview mirror now, I realise the road did not just take me to a job. It carried me through a season of unravelling and rebuilding, mile after mile, until I could finally see myself with a clarity I hadn't known before. The road held my questions, my grief, my doubts, and my quiet hopes, and somewhere along those long stretches of tarmac, something in me shifted.

It took me to myself.

Not the version shaped by titles or expectations, not the one performing strength while quietly breaking, but the person beneath all of that, the one I had forgotten how to recognise. And that, more than anything, is the destination I did not know I was searching for. I thought I was driving toward a new job, a new chapter, a new beginning. But what I found was far more profound: a return to who I truly was, and who I was becoming.

The road didn't give me answers. It gave me back my own voice. It gave me space to breathe, to grieve, to hope again. And in that space, I discovered that sometimes the journey we fear the most is the one that leads us home to ourselves.

And so, I leave this journey with hope. Hope that whoever reads these words will know that healing is possible. That laughter can return. That singing without shame is a kind of prayer. That grace can find us anywhere, even on the road, even in the driver's seat, even when we least expect it.

Because I did not just survive grief. I drove through it. And somewhere along the way, I began to live again.

CHAPTER 15

The Road Ahead

The journey doesn't end; it transforms. In the rearview mirror of grief, we glimpse grace, and ahead, the open road of healing stretches endlessly.

When I look back now, the road feels like a thread that stitched together the torn fabric of my life. It didn't mend the tears perfectly, grief never allows for that, but it held the pieces long enough for me to begin weaving them into something new. The road did not erase the losses; I still miss my son's anticipated innocent questions, the ones that would have tumbled out of him with such earnest curiosity. I still miss my father's laughter, that deep, familiar sound that could steady me even on the worst days. I still miss my mother's gentle wisdom, the way she could offer comfort with just a look.

And then there is my Mami Nta'ambang, her nurturing love, her quiet strength, the way she cared without hesitation. I miss her in a way that aches differently, because I know I will never have the chance to reciprocate the love she poured into me. That realisation carries its own kind of grief, a longing not just for her presence but for the opportunity to give back what she so freely gave.

I miss my uncle's wisdom too, the thoughtful conversations, the depth of insight he carried so effortlessly. I had dreamed of collaborating with him on a book project one day, of capturing his brilliance on paper. That dream now lives only in memory, a reminder of the stories we never got to tell together.

And of course, I miss the steady reassurance of Bo Paul, whose presence had a way of grounding me, reminding me that I wasn't navigating life alone. His absence still echoes in the quiet moments.

These losses remain. They sit beside me, not as weights meant to crush me but as reminders of the love that shaped me. And the road taught me something profound: healing does not mean forgetting. It does not ask you to silence the ache or pretend the longing isn't there. Healing means learning to carry the love and the loss together, without letting them break you. It means allowing grief to walk with you without letting it lead. It means recognising that the weight you carry is not a burden to escape but a testament to the depth of the connections that made you who you are.

The road didn't take the pain away. It simply showed me that I could keep moving with it, that I could live with both the sorrow and the grace, and that somehow, in the midst of it all, I could still become whole.

I began this journey broken, driving through miles of grief and uncertainty. I didn't set out with a map or a plan; I simply kept moving because staying still felt impossible. I thought I was escaping, running from the pain, the memories, the version of myself I no longer recognised. But somewhere along those long stretches of motorway, I realised I wasn't running away at all. I was moving toward something. Toward grace. Toward peace. Toward a version of myself I did not know existed, one shaped not by achievement or expectation but by resilience, tenderness, and truth.

Each mile became a lesson in its own quiet way. The road taught me that healing rarely arrives with clarity; it comes in whispers, in pauses, in the steady rhythm of tyres on tarmac. Each horizon reminded me that life keeps going even when we feel stuck, even when grief convinces us we've reached the end of ourselves. The world didn't stop because I was hurting, and slowly, gently, I learned that I didn't have to stop either.

And so must we. Not in a way that denies the pain or rushes the process, but in the simple, courageous act of taking the next step, the next breath, the next mile. Because sometimes moving forward is not about strength; it's about trust, trust that the road will hold us, trust that grace will meet us, trust that we are becoming someone new with every turn of the wheel.

The road ahead is still long. I know that now more than ever. There will be detours that pull me off course, potholes that jolt me back into old fears, and unexpected turns that force me to slow down and pay attention. But I no longer fear them. I've learned that the road rarely unfolds the way we imagine, and that this unpredictability is not a threat, it's an invitation.

I have learned that detours can lead to discoveries, to places I never would have found if life had gone according to plan. I've learned that broken roads can still take you home, even when the journey feels uneven and uncertain. And I've learned that grace often waits in the places we least expect, in the quiet moments when we think we've lost our way, in the gentle reminders that appear when we're ready to see them, sometimes in the rearview mirror, sometimes just beyond the next bend.

The road ahead may twist and rise and fall, but I carry with me the assurance that I am no longer walking, or driving, blind. I have been reshaped by the miles behind me, steadied by the lessons they offered, and softened by the grace that met me along the way. Whatever comes next, I know I can face it. Not because the road will be easy, but because I am no longer afraid of where it might lead.

If you are reading this and carrying your own grief, your own loss, your own uncertainty, I want you to know this: you are not alone. Even if it feels like the world has moved on while you remain suspended in your pain, even if the silence around you feels deafening, even if you can't yet see a way forward, you are not walking this road by yourself.

The road may feel endless, stretching out in front of you with no clear destination, but healing happens in motion. Not in grand leaps, not in sudden breakthroughs, but in the small, steady acts of continuing. Keep driving. Keep breathing. Keep taking the next step, even if it's slow, even if it's shaky. Healing doesn't demand perfection; it asks only for presence.

Keep looking for grace in the ordinary. It's there, even when grief tries to convince you otherwise. It's in the sunlight breaking through clouds on a day you thought would be nothing but grey. It's in the kindness of strangers who hold the door, offer a smile, or simply exist gently in your world. It's in the quiet strength you did not know you had, the strength that gets you out of bed, that carries you through another hour, that whispers, *You're still here. You're still moving.*

Grace doesn't always arrive with pomp. Sometimes it slips in softly, unnoticed at first, until one day you realise it has been holding you all along. Carry gratitude for where you have been and let hope guide you toward where you are going. The journey is yours now to shape, to stumble through, to celebrate. Walk it with openness, knowing that even the smallest steps ripple outward, shaping the future in ways you cannot yet see.

The road ahead is not perfect, but it is possible. And that is enough. I no longer expect the journey to be smooth or predictable; life has taught me that certainty is a luxury, not a guarantee. There will be days when the path feels uneven, when doubt creeps in, when old wounds ache without warning. But possibility, however small, however fragile, is still a kind of hope.

I've learned that "possible" is its own kind of promise. It means there is room to grow, room to heal, room to become. It means the future is not closed off, even if it looks different from what I once imagined. And sometimes, enough doesn't look like triumph or clarity. Sometimes enough is simply the courage to keep moving, to trust the next step, to believe that even an imperfect road can lead somewhere meaningful.

The road may not be flawless, but it is open. And open is enough for now.

CHAPTER 16

Back to the Question...

Can Healing Happen in Motion?

Healing is often imagined as stillness, a quiet room, a soft pause amid life's chaos, a retreat into silence where the world finally stops long enough for the heart to catch up. We picture it as a gentle exhale, a moment of clarity, a sanctuary untouched by noise or movement. And sometimes healing does look like that. But more often, the deeper truth is that healing happens in motion. It happens on the road, in the journey, in the act of moving forward, even when the pieces of your life still feel scattered.

It happens when you're driving through the night with tears drying on your cheeks, when the hum of the engine becomes the only steady thing you can hold onto. It happens when you keep going, not because you feel strong, but because stopping feels impossible. Healing unfolds in the rhythm of tyres on tarmac, in the shifting landscapes outside your window, in the simple act of choosing to move, even when brokenness remains.

Motion does not oppose healing; it becomes the very way through which grace enters. Grace slips in between the miles, in the moments when you least expect it, when the wind rushes through an open window, when the horizon widens, when your breath steadies without you noticing. Healing is not the absence of movement; it is the quiet transformation that happens because you kept going.

In biblical narratives, we witness healing repeatedly in moments of motion. It is striking how often restoration unfolds not in stillness, but in the act of going, walking, reaching, or obeying a call that requires movement. Some of these well-known examples include, but are not limited to:

The Israelites in Exodus: Healing from slavery did not happen in Egypt's stillness but during their long, uncertain march through the wilderness. Their restoration unfolded not in comfort, but in motion, step after step across unfamiliar terrain. As they walked, wandered, complained, trusted, doubted, and returned to God, their identity was slowly reshaped. They were no longer a people defined by oppression but a people learning, often painfully, what it meant to be free. Their healing was not a single moment of deliverance at the Red Sea; it was a journey of becoming, forged in the dust of the desert and the daily act of moving forward even when they did not know where the road would lead.

The Woman with the Issue of Blood (Mark 5:25–34): Her healing occurred not in a temple or a clinic, but in the midst of a bustling, chaotic crowd. She had spent twelve long years suffering, twelve years of disappointment, isolation, and exhaustion, yet she still found the courage to move.

She pushed through bodies and barriers, through shame and weakness, through the weight of her own history. She reached out while in motion, stretching her hand toward Jesus as He walked, believing that even the briefest touch could change everything. And it did. Her restoration came not in stillness, but in the act of reaching, pressing, and moving forward despite her pain. Her healing was born in motion, an embodied faith that refused to stay still.

The Road to Emmaus (Luke 24:13–35): Two disciples, heavy with grief after the crucifixion, did not encounter the risen Christ while sitting still in their sorrow. They met Him on the road, in the midst of their walking, their questioning, their confusion. Their despair began to shift not in a static shrine or a sacred chamber, but in the rhythm of footsteps and conversation. As they moved, they processed their pain; as they walked, they made space for revelation. Christ joined them in motion, unrecognised at first, matching their pace, listening to their grief, gently opening their understanding. By the time they reached their destination, their hearts were burning with a hope they thought they had lost. Their healing came through the journey itself, through the act of moving forward even when they did not yet know resurrection was walking beside them.

St Paul's Journeys: Saul, who later became St Paul, his letters and teachings were not born from a life rooted in one place, but from the constant motion of travel, dusty roads, crowded ports, unpredictable seas, and long stretches of walking from one community to another. The gospel spread through movement, carried on his footsteps as he crossed regions, cultures, and languages. Along the way, communities were healed, encouraged, corrected, and transformed as he moved from town to town. His ministry was shaped not by stillness but by the rhythm of going, writing from prisons, preaching in marketplaces, reasoning in synagogues, and strengthening believers wherever he found them. Paul's life reminds us that spiritual growth often unfolds on the road, and that transformation can happen in the very act of moving toward others with purpose and conviction.

Similarly, the lives of the mystics demonstrate a familiar path. Their stories echo the same truth found in Scripture: that transformation rarely happens in stillness alone. Whether wandering through deserts, journeying across continents, or walking the quiet paths of their own inner landscapes, mystics throughout history discovered God not by remaining rooted in one place, but by allowing themselves to be led, sometimes gently, sometimes through upheaval, into motion. Their healing, their revelations, and their deepening intimacy with the divine unfolded as they moved, questioned, surrendered, and followed the faintest whisper of grace into unfamiliar territory.

St. Augustine: In his *Confessions*, Augustine describes life as a restless journey toward God, a movement that began long before he recognised it. His healing was not a sudden moment of enlightenment but a pilgrimage of the soul, marked by wandering, questioning, resisting, and finally surrendering. He speaks of his heart as "restless" until it found its rest in God, a rest that emerged only after years of searching through philosophies, ambitions, and desires that could never satisfy him. Augustine's transformation unfolded through motion: the inner motion of wrestling with truth, the outward motion of leaving behind old ways of living, and the spiritual motion of turning, slowly, painfully, beautifully, toward the One who had been pursuing him all along. For Augustine, healing was not an event; it was a lifelong journey of becoming, guided by grace step by step.

Meister Eckhart: He was a 13th–14th-century German Dominican theologian, philosopher, and mystic, renowned for his teachings on the soul's union with God and the transformative power of detachment. He asserted that detachment and union with God often arise through the "flowing" of life, with motion representing surrender and movement signifying openness to the divine presence.

Rumi: A 13th-century Persian poet, Islamic scholar, and Sufi mystic whose writings on love, longing, and union with the divine made him one of the most influential spiritual voices in history. The Sufi poet saw motion as dance, the whirling of the dervish as a metaphor for healing through surrender. "Try to accept the changing seasons of your heart," he wrote, reminding us that healing is found in the turning, not resisting.

Building on the mystics, several philosophical reflections also seem to confirm that there is healing in motion. Across centuries and cultures, thinkers have observed that transformation rarely occurs in stagnation. Instead, it unfolds through movement, physical, emotional, intellectual, or spiritual. Philosophers have long suggested that clarity emerges not from remaining fixed in one place, but from engaging with the world, walking through questions, and allowing experience to reshape understanding. Their insights echo the same truth found in Scripture and in the lives of the mystics: that healing is not merely a destination but a dynamic process, one that reveals itself as we move, explore, and grow.

Heraclitus: The pre-Socratic Greek philosopher believed that change is the fundamental nature of reality. His famous saying, "No man ever steps in the same river twice," illustrates that everything is constantly in motion.

Aristotle: Aristotle, one of the greatest philosophers of all time, discussed energeia, the activity of being fully alive. Healing is not a passive state but an active engagement with life's ongoing process. Aristotle taught that everything exists in a state of potential (what it could become) and actuality (what it is). Motion is the process through which potential becomes actual. Healing as Becoming: Illness, grief, or brokenness represent a state of potential, incomplete and unfinished. Healing involves the movement towards actuality, towards wholeness. For Aristotle, motion is not merely physical movement but the unfolding of being itself. To live is to be in motion, to realise what is possible.

Nietzsche: Even the German philosopher, cultural critic, and poet, best known for his radical critiques of religion, morality, and truth, would likely argue that healing in progress is not only possible but vital, because life itself is a continual process of becoming, struggle, and transformation. In his radical philosophy, movement is fundamental. The concept of "becoming" rather than "being" implies that healing is an ongoing process, a shift towards wholeness rather than a fixed goal.

Healing on the Drive! The drive itself, as a metaphor for motion, becomes the sacred space where grief, grace, and healing converge. It is not merely a stretch of road but a moving sanctuary, a place where the heart can unravel, breathe, and slowly reassemble itself. As the wheels turn, something within us shifts too, often quietly, almost imperceptibly.

Grief is carried with us, but it changes shape as the scenery changes. What feels unbearable at the start of the journey softens mile by mile, not because the loss disappears, but because motion gives it room to settle differently within us. The landscape outside the window becomes a mirror for the landscape within, valleys of sorrow, hills of memory, long plains of reflection. And somehow, in the rhythm of the drive, grief loosens its grip just enough for us to keep going.

Grace meets us unexpectedly, slipping into the journey like a roadside encounter or a stranger's kindness. It appears in the way sunlight breaks through a canopy of trees, in the sudden clarity that arrives between songs on the radio, in the quiet reassurance that rises unbidden from somewhere deep. Grace does not always announce itself; sometimes it simply sits beside us in the passenger seat, steady and unassuming, reminding us that we are held even when we feel lost.

Healing is not a final destination but a gradual transformation that occurs between departure and arrival. It unfolds in the in-between spaces, the pauses at traffic lights, the long stretches of open road, the moments when we realise we are breathing a little easier than before. Healing happens not because we have reached the end of the journey, but because we dared to begin it, to stay in motion, to trust that the road itself has something to teach us.

So, can healing happen while in motion? The answer is yes, profoundly, repeatedly, and mysteriously. Healing is not only possible in motion; it often depends on it. The act of moving forward, even if limping or uncertain, becomes the very ground where grace meets grief and transforms into healing. Healing is not the end of the road; it is the road itself.

CHAPTER 17

Grief, Grace and the Ongoing Journey

On every road we travel, grief rides with us, but so does grace,
and that's why we keep going.

There is a point on every long drive when the road behind you becomes a kind of memory. You can't see the exact bends anymore, nor the potholes that rattled your bones, nor the stretches where the sun poured through the windscreen like a blessing. But you know they're there. You know you've travelled them. You know they've shaped the way you hold the wheel now.

And perhaps that is the quiet truth of life: we are always driving with a rear-view mirror full of moments that made us, moments that marked us, including moments that left their fingerprints on our hearts. Some of those moments were joyful, others painful. Some were loud and unforgettable; others slipped in unnoticed, only to reveal their significance years later. But all of them, in their own way, became part of our journey.

As I look back on the road we've travelled together in these pages, I'm struck by how grief, grace, and healing weave themselves into the everyday. Not as grand, dramatic events, but as subtle companions on the drive. They sit with us, sometimes quietly, sometimes insistently, sometimes uncomfortably. They shape the way we see the world, the way we love, the way we hope.

And so, as we approach the end of this book, I want to linger a little longer on the road metaphor, not because it is neat or poetic, but because it is true. Life is a drive. A long, unpredictable, beautiful, exhausting, grace-filled drive. And every one of us is navigating it the best we can.

The Everyday Griefs We Carry

When people hear the word grief, they often think of funerals, of deep losses, of the kind of sorrow that knocks the breath out of your lungs. And yes, that is grief. But grief is also quieter than that. It is more ordinary. It is threaded through the fabric of daily life.

There are the small griefs, the ones we rarely name. The disappointment that lingers after a conversation that didn't go the way you hoped. The ache of watching a child grow up too quickly. The heaviness of realising a friendship has drifted. The sting of a dream that no longer fits. The fatigue of carrying responsibilities that no one sees.

These are the griefs that punctuate our days like speed bumps, small, jarring reminders that life is not always smooth. They slow us down. They make us pay attention. They remind us that we are human, that we feel deeply, that we care.

And then there are the larger griefs, the ones that shake the foundations of our world. The loss of someone we love. The betrayal we didn't see coming. The sudden or long-drawn divorce and the diagnosis that changes everything. The tragedy arrives without warning, like a sudden storm on an open road.

We live in a world where tragedy is never far away. Natural disasters devastate communities. Acts of violence shatter lives. Injustice persists. Human cruelty leaves scars that span generations. And sometimes, the weight of it all feels unbearable.

But here is the truth that sits quietly beneath the grief: we are not meant to carry it alone.

The Grace That Finds Us

Grace is one of those words that can feel abstract until you experience it. But once you do, you recognise it everywhere. It comes in many shapes, forms and flavours, such as the unexpected kindness that arrives when you are at your lowest. It is the friend who shows up with food when you haven't had the strength to cook. It is the family member who listens without judgment. It is the colleague who covers for you when your heart is too heavy to function. It is the stranger who smiles at you in a moment when you feel invisible.

Grace is the warmth of a hand on your shoulder. The text message that says, "Thinking of you." The laughter that breaks through your tears. The quiet moment of peace that comes after a long night of wrestling with your thoughts.

Grace is not always loud. It does not always announce itself. Sometimes it is as subtle as the way the light falls through the trees on a morning when you thought you couldn't get out of bed. Sometimes it is as gentle as the sound of someone breathing beside you, reminding you that you are not alone.

Grace is a reminder that even in a world full of tragedy, goodness still exists. There are still people who care. There are still moments of beauty that catch you off guard. There are still reasons to hope.

And grace does something else: it helps us heal.

Healing as a Journey, Not a Destination

Healing is not a straight road. It is not a neat process. It is not something you can schedule or control. Healing is a journey that winds, loops, stalls, and surprises you.

Some days, healing feels like progress. You wake with a little more strength. You laugh without forcing it. You find yourself singing along to a song you used to love. You notice the world looks a little brighter. On other days, healing feels like going backwards. The grief returns with a force you didn't expect. The sadness sits heavy on your chest. The memories sting. The road feels long and lonely.

But both kinds of days are part of the journey

Healing is not about forgetting. It is not about pretending the pain never existed. It is about learning to carry the pain differently. It is about allowing the grief to soften rather than harden you. It is about letting grace seep into the cracks. Healing is the courage to keep driving even when the road is unclear. It is the willingness to trust that the journey is worth continuing. It is the quiet decision, made again and again, to move forward.

And healing is rarely something we do alone. It is something we do in community, in the presence of those who love us, support us, and remind us of who we are when we forget.

The World Moves On, and So Do We

One of the hardest truths about grief is that the world does not stop for it. The traffic keeps flowing. The days keep passing. The seasons keep changing. People keep living their lives. At first, this can feel cruel. How can the world continue when yours has been shattered? How can people laugh, work, celebrate, and carry on as though nothing has happened?

But over time, this truth becomes something else. It becomes a kind of mercy. Because the world moving on is not a sign that your grief is insignificant. It is a sign that life is resilient. It is a sign that joy still exists. It is a sign that healing is possible.

And eventually, you find yourself moving with the world again. Not because you have forgotten, but because you have grown. Not because the pain has vanished, but because you have learned to live with it. Not because the road has become easier, but because you have become stronger.

The world moves on, and so do we. And in that movement, there is hope.

Hope as a Companion on the Drive

Hope is not naive optimism. It is not pretending everything is fine. It is not ignoring the reality of pain. Hope is the quiet belief that the story is not over. It is the conviction that there is still goodness ahead. It is the trust that even in the darkest night, the dawn will come.

Hope is the companion who sits beside you on the drive, whispering, "Keep going." Hope is the voice that says, "There is more to see." Hope is the gentle nudge that encourages you to roll down the window, breathe in the fresh air, and notice the beauty around you.

Hope does not erase grief. But it gives you the strength to carry it. Hope does not eliminate pain. But it gives you the courage to face it. Hope does not guarantee an easy road. But it promises that the journey is worth taking.

And hope is contagious. When you carry it, others feel it. When you live with hope, you become a source of grace for those around you. You become the person who helps someone else heal. You become the light on someone else's dark road.

Looking Back, Looking Forward

As we come to the end of this book, I want to invite you to pause. To look in the rear-view mirror. To acknowledge the road you've travelled, not just in these pages, but in your life. Think of the griefs you've carried. The losses you've endured. The disappointments that shaped you. The moments that broke you open.

Think of the graces you've received. The people who stood by you. The kindnesses that lifted you. The unexpected joys that reminded you of the beauty of being alive. Think of the healing that has taken place, slowly, quietly, imperfectly. Think of the strength you've gained. The wisdom you've earned. The resilience that now lives in your bones. And then, look ahead.

The road stretches out before you, unmapped, unpredictable, full of possibility. There will be challenges. There will be grief. There will be moments when you feel lost. But there will also be grace. There will be healing. There will be beauty you cannot yet imagine. There will be people who walk with you, support you, and love you. There will be reasons to hope.

You have travelled far. You have endured much. You have grown in ways you may not even realise. And you are ready for the road ahead.

The Journey Continues

So take a deep breath. Adjust your mirrors. Set your hands on the wheel. You are not alone on this drive. You never have been. You never will be. Grief will visit you, yes. But so will grace. Healing will come, slowly but surely. And hope will guide you, even when the night is long.

The world is full of tragedy, but it is also full of wonder. It is full of cruelty, but also full of kindness. It is full of endings, but also full of beginnings. And you are part of that story. You are part of the beauty, the resilience, the courage that keep the world moving forward.

So keep driving. Keep hoping. Keep healing. Keep noticing the grace that surrounds you. Keep offering grace to others. Keep living with a heart that is open, tender, and brave. The journey is not over. And you are ready for whatever comes next.

Healing in Motion

We do not heal only in silence.
We heal in footsteps, in journeys, in the turning of wheels.
We heal while the road hums beneath us,
while grief rides in the passenger seat,
While grace waits at the next bend.

The Israelites found their freedom not in Egypt's stillness,
But in the wilderness march,
Dust rising, hearts reshaping,
Identity reborn in motion.

The woman reached for Jesus in the press of the crowd,
Her hand trembling, her body moving,
And healing came as He walked.

Two disciples met the risen Christ.
Not in a shrine, but on the road to Emmaus
Their sorrow lifted with each step,
Their hope rekindled in the rhythm of walking.

Mystics have whispered the same truth:
Augustine's restless heart,
Eckhart's flowing surrender,
Rumi's whirling dance
All speak of healing found in movement,
In the turning, in the becoming.

Philosophers remind us:
Heraclitus' river never still,
Aristotle's life as activity,
Nietzsche's becoming,
All point to motion as the ground of transformation.

And so, the drive itself becomes holy.
Grief travels with us,
But shifts as the scenery changes.
Grace surprises us,
A roadside kindness, a sudden light.
Healing does not wait at the destination.
It is the road itself.

Yes, healing can happen in motion.
It happens in the limping forward,
In the uncertain step,
In the courage to keep driving
When the night feels endless.

Healing is not the end of the road.
Healing is the road.
And as long as we move,
Grace moves with us.

G. N. Angafor

Acknowledgements

No journey through grief, grace, and healing is ever walked alone. Though the road was often rough, I was blessed with companions who stood by me, encouraged me, and reminded me that even in brokenness, there is beauty, and even in weakness, there is strength.

First and foremost, I would like to thank my wife, Claris, who has always been my anchor, especially in the stormy seas explored in *Grief, Grace, and Healing on the Drive*. My children, Christabel, Lesra, and Gicles, your love, patience, and unwavering presence have ensured that I was held and supported through the most difficult moments. You stood by me when silence felt overwhelming, and your care gave me the courage to keep moving forward.

To my friend, mentor, and elder brother, Fr. Victor Forgho, I owe you a profound debt of gratitude. Thank you for writing an exceptionally spiritual and reflective foreword for this book. You helped me navigate the challenging task of organising my mother's funeral, offering wisdom and strength when I felt most vulnerable. You also kindly offered to conduct the wake-keep Mass and were the main celebrant at the funeral Mass. Your guidance was a beacon of light in a time of darkness.

I am also grateful to my friends and colleagues who listened when I first shared the concept of *Grief, Grace, and Healing on the Drive.* Your encouragement gave me the confidence to pursue this work. Special thanks to Ivan and Denis, who took the time to proofread the original manuscript and helped shape these words into what they are today. I equally appreciate the input from my younger brother and family head of the Ndzamngang dynasty, Mr Moses Abongbuh (Pa Ndzamngang), for combing through the original manuscript and reminding me of some important details about my auntie and uncle's stories that I had left out.

I am deeply grateful to my elder brother, *Tsehfor* Dr Mathias Alubafi, for not only reviewing the original manuscript but also encouraging me with the confidence that it was of publishable quality.

To my publisher, Dr Jude Fokwang and the team at Spears Books, thank you for your patience, guidance, and belief in this project. Your support has made it possible for these reflections to reach readers.

Finally, I want to acknowledge you, the reader. I hope that within these pages you will find companionship, comfort, and the reassurance that grief does not lessen love, that grace can find us in the most unexpected places, and that healing, though gradual, can surprise us with its quiet strength. This book is just as much yours as it is mine.

May it serve as a reminder that the journey, although challenging, is never undertaken alone.

About the Author

Giddeon N. Angafor, PhD, is a cybersecurity scholar, lecturer, and cultural leader whose life bridges the technical and the deeply human domains. He holds a PhD in Computing with a specialisation in cybersecurity, supported by advanced studies in Security Management, Education and Philosophy. His academic work includes peer-reviewed research articles on cyber incident-response training, game-based learning, information security and privacy, and AI-related scams, developed through affiliations with institutions including De Montfort University, the Alan Turing Institute, the University of Winchester, and the University of Greater Manchester, all in the UK.

Dr Angafor's professional journey spans education, private and public sector IT, and cybersecurity, including serving as an IT Security Analyst within UK law enforcement. He currently lectures in Computer Science (Cybersecurity) at the School of Arts and Creative Technologies, the University of Greater Manchester.

Beyond academia, he carries the distinguished cultural title of *Akhamenchwo* (King's representative), serving as the Bambui Fon's representative to the United Kingdom and Mainland Europe. In this role, he works to preserve and promote the heritage and communal identity of the Bambui people, fostering unity and cultural continuity across the diaspora.

A husband, father, grandfather, and lifelong student of the human experience, Dr Angafor writes with a blend of analytical clarity and emotional depth. His reflections on love, loss, resilience, and renewal shape the heart of *Grief, Grace, and Healing on the Drive*, offering readers a narrative that is both personal and universally resonant.

About the Publisher

Spears Books is an independent publisher dedicated to providing innovative publication strategies with emphasis on Africana stories and perspectives. As a platform for alternative voices, we prioritize the accessibility and affordability of our titles to ensure that relevant and often marginal voices are represented in the global marketplace of ideas. Our titles – poetry, fiction, narrative nonfiction, memoirs, reference, travel writing, African languages, and young people's literature – aim to bring African worldviews closer to diverse readers. Our titles are distributed in paperback and electronic formats globally by African Books Collective.

Connect with Us: Go to www.spearsbooks.org to learn about exclusive previews and read excerpts of new books, find detailed information on our titles, authors, subject area books, and special discounts.

Subscribe to our Free Newsletter: Be amongst the first to hear about our newest publications, special discount offers, news about bestsellers, author interviews, coupons and more! Subscribe to our newsletter by visiting www.spearsbooks.org

Quantity Discounts: Spears Books are available at quantity discounts for orders of ten or more copies. Contact Spears Books at orders@spearsmedia.com.

Host a Reading Group: Learn more about how to host a reading group on our website at www.spearsbooks.org

www.ingramcontent.com/pod-product-compliance
Lightning Source LLC
Chambersburg PA
CBHW022103050726
47591CB00002B/647